LAST OF HIS KIND.

OLD TEA-CLIPPER CAPTAIN'S DEATH.

Captain Andrew Shewan, the last survivor of the old tea-clipper captains, was buried yesterday at Ealing. He was 78 years of age, and came of an old seafaring family of peterhead. His grandfather died from exposure on an ice floe in Greenland in 1830.

Captain Shewan first went to seat in 1860 on the Chaa-Sze, and at the age of 23 succeeded his father as captain of the Norman Court. He soon became renowned for his seamanship, and in 1872 made a memorable run liome from China in the then "record" time of 95 days. On several occasions his ship ran foul of Chinese pirates.

He was a frequent contributor to shipping journals, and was the author of a book of reminiscences called "The Great Days of Sail."

Sunday Times. Dec 18 '27

*Honor Ramsden.
with Mother's love.
Xmces 1927.*

THE GREAT DAYS OF SAIL

SOME REMINISCENCES OF A TEA-CLIPPER CAPTAIN

BY

ANDREW SHEWAN

Late Master of the " Norman Court "

EDITED BY

REX CLEMENTS

Author of "A Gipsy of the Horn," "A Stately Southerner," etc.

HEATH CRANTON LIMITED

6 FLEET LANE   **LONDON E.C.4**

1927

Printed in Great Britain for Heath Cranton Limited by
Northumberland Press Limited, Newcastle-on-Tyne

"The ocean knows no favourites. Her bounty is reserved for those who have the wit to learn her secrets, the courage to bear her buffets, and the will to persist, through good fortune and ill, in her rugged service."

—SAMUEL ELIOT MORISON.

FOREWORD

THE ocean-going sailing-ship has almost disappeared, and it serves to remind us how brief was the culminating era of the clippers that the following reminiscences are those of a man yet alive who shared in their heyday, and whose early recollections are of the first Aberdeen-built vessels which, in the fifties, wrested the blue ribbon of the world's carrying trade from the famous American flyers of Boston and New York. Within the span of a single human life the clipper-ship era is almost wholly contained.

In his own person Captain Shewan sums up that era. Coming of an old seafaring family of Peterhead, he speaks with understanding and authority. His grandfather was a whaling captain who died as far back as 1830, through exposure on an ice-floe, his ship being nipped in the Greenland ice. His father, becoming master of a schooner in the St. John's fish trade at the age of twenty-one, rose to the command of that early "crack," the *Lammermuir,* and afterwards of the *Norman Court.*

Captain Shewan himself made his first voyage to sea in the *Chaa-sze* in 1860, and followed his father in command of the *Norman Court.* He is to-day probably the last survivor of the tea-clipper captains who, in the sixties and seventies of last century, added one of the most striking and picturesque chapters to British maritime history.

9

His memories have an interest and his opinions a weight to which few seaman-authors can lay claim. What those of us whose seafaring began with the century know about the tea-clippers of the halcyon age of sail, we know almost entirely from the written or the printed word. At best our information is from the yarns of old shipmates who loved to remember the feats of their youth.

But Captain Shewan knew the ships whose names are now almost household words as one can only know the intimate associates of a lifetime. Brought up in Blackwall of the old days, his knowledge of the clippers is from first-hand experience, his judgments from professional estimates formed at the time. He has been on board almost every one of the British clippers he mentions and raced with many of them on the high seas. It is Cæsar who tells the story of his own wars.

There has of late been much interest displayed in sailing-ships and the vanished way of life connected with them. Now, before they pass into the limbo of forgotten things, it seems fitting that one among the best-known of those skilful and daring commanders of the great days of sail should add his share to the stock of material available for those who, in future, would learn something of a great epoch in our naval annals.

REX CLEMENTS.

Photo. by W. Whiffen, Poplar, E.

BLACKWALL IN TEA CLIPPER DAYS.

Facing p. 10

CONTENTS

LIST OF ILLUSTRATIONS

CHAPTER I

EARLY DAYS

So much has been written of late concerning life at sea when our overseas trade was carried on without the aid of steam, and merchants relied solely for transport on the wings of the wind, that I hesitate to add to the total. Yet, as a sailor's son, myself a sailor, brought up from childhood amid sailor surroundings, with sailor relatives and friends, I must plead the love of all lore pertaining to the almost extinct " windjammers " as my excuse for venturing on the well-worn theme.

As a boy my home, in the fifties of last century, was in Stepney. Most of my schoolmates and associates were sons of seafaring men, and our outlook was to the sea.

It would nearly always happen that one or other of our fathers' ships was on the homeward-bound list, and almost any tide we had hopes of seeing the *Lammermuir, John Temperley, Pride of the Ocean,* or other famous ship, looming up over the fleet of barges in Woolwich Reach, like a Triton amongst minnows.

Each of us well knew the distinctive marks of the vessel that claimed our particular interest, and excitement ran high when " our ship " was seen in the river, shortening in the rope or swinging to the flood, preparatory to dropping alongside the landing-stage in readiness to enter the East India Dock.

But time and tide wait for no man, and sometimes " our ship " docked at night or unexpectedly. One might have waited many days in hope deferred, and, after all, the " long awa' " ship be hauled into dock ere one was aware of it.

Yet that did not often happen. In those days a maritime register was published weekly, giving a list of all ships homeward bound to the United Kingdom. As soon as the departure of a vessel from a foreign port was posted up at " Lloyd's," or in the " Jerusalem " (an old-time coffee-house used as an exchange by the shipping folk in the city of London), the fact was entered in the register. Later, should the vessel be spoken at sea or reported as having passed any particular point of land, such information was added to the record. Thus a glance at the *List* would inform one when and where any ship was last heard of.

My father's ship being in the China trade, our first notification would be " Left Whampoa " or " Macao," as the case might be, on a certain date. A week or two later this would be altered and the legend would read : " Passed Anjer "—a Java town in the Straits of Sunda. Though the tea-clippers, homeward bound, seldom anchored at Anjer, there were always Malay boats cruising in the Narrows, from which ships were able to obtain supplies of fowls, fruit, etc., and whose skippers were in duty bound to report each ship they boarded to the Dutch port-captain ashore. These reports were sent regularly to Lloyd's, and it was seldom a vessel passed Anjer without notice.

Then, after a longer interval, we would look for the welcome : " Passed St. Helena." This island lay right in the track of all ships rounding the Cape of Good Hope, and those that did not call for a supply of water or vegetables would unfailingly " make their number " if they passed the island during the hours of daylight.

As, however, the mail steamer only called at the island once a month and took another month to come home, it often happened that smart ships were in London before such reports of them arrived.

Our particular ship, the *Lammermuir*, being a "heeler," it was most unlikely that any vessel should speak with her at sea and be in London river before her. Yet as the time drew near when it was reasonable to expect she was nearing the Channel, *Lloyd's List* was eagerly scanned for news. Every beer-shop and public-house along the river from Wapping to Blackwall took in one or more copies of the paper, which were lent out to customers, "not to be kept more than ten minutes by any one household."

Once indoors, the coveted *List* was spread out on the table and each of the signalling-points down Channel —the Lizard, Start Point and the rest—quickly scanned for the well-known name. "Deal" was the last place that interested us, for, if the ship were posted at "Gravesend," father would be home before we could see it in the *List*.

Keen interest, too, was taken in the direction of the wind and state of the weather. Quite contented when the reports had anything with a "W" in it, we pulled long faces when the dreaded "east" appeared. This means little to maritime folk nowadays—at most a few hours' delay—but in windjammer times a spell of easterly winds made the import quays bare of shipping and brought hard fare to dockers, riggers and other waterside labourers. Even the comparatively aristocratic shipwrights and lightermen felt the pinch of a long-continued "easterly," which, like the proverbial cat, was said to be gifted with nine lives. As an Irish sailor complained, "Six weeks of aisterly winds in the month of March" was no joke for ships beating up the English Channel.

B

On one occasion, in February, 1866, I have vivid recollections of leaving the Downs with the first faint air of an " easterly " which carried us to Madeira in eight days, and thereafter continued almost persistently for nine or ten weeks; with such evil effects to many homeward-bounders, short of provisions after long voyages, that the Admiralty sent cruisers with stores and water to relieve those vessels which were held so far to the westward they could not fetch into an Irish port.

In October, 1871, again, in the tea-clipper *Norman Court*, we arrived at Blackwall—the first ship to dock there for over three weeks. The pier was crowded with " out of works," who gave us welcome as a harbinger of hope, for now they could look for further vessels. Even the crimps from the Highway were hard hit, and when the ship tied up in the Basin there were free fights among them for possession of the sailors' chests. Jack was bound to follow the boarding-house runner who had his " dunnage."

Oft times, during easterly winds, a telegram landed by a hoveller at some port down Channel would be the first intimation of the approach of the long-awaited ship; to be followed perhaps by a note from a friendly shipbroker, telling us that the *Lammermuir* in tow had passed through the Downs at such and such an hour, bound for the river.

The foreign-going shipmaster usually left his ship at Gravesend to facilitate her entry at the custom-house. Father, therefore, might be expected home any minute, and we boys hung about Stepney railway station on the look-out for a sunburnt seaman, with flowing moustaches and majestic beard, who, if not " full of strange oaths," yet commanded a voice and bearing that made him conspicuous among the pale-faced Londoners of those days.

At length the happy hour arrived, and with father ensconced in the armchair, a neighbour or two in for company (haply a mariner's wife, anxious for news of her good man), we listened open-mouthed to tales of tea-carrying rivals being " out-manœuvred, out-weathered and out-sailed," of ships spoken at sea and of heavy squalls off Borneo. Or we were thrilled at hearing of narrow squeaks of collision, of making the land and picking up the pilot—all happenings trivial enough to ancient mariners, but to us boys " the vision splendid."

We heard of the welfare of our friends in the ship's company, and noted particulars of any monkeys, mongooses, parrots, Java sparrows or such-like, as well as Chinese toys, dragon kites and preserved ginger, brought home for our delectation. Best news of all, the *Lammermuir*, we would hear, was to dock at Blackwall next forenoon, and the two eldest boys were to miss school and be on the pierhead to meet her.

Instead of a subdued and somewhat anxious household, we had laughter and jollity; and Liza, our maid-of-all-work, with visions of handsome apprentices adorning her back kitchen, moved round " as busy," as father said, " as the devil in a gale of wind."

Meeting the ship next day was an event to be long remembered. As " the captain's children " we were persons of consequence, to be hoisted aboard when the ship sheered alongside the " dummy " and to be made a fuss of by the kindly mate and steward. Even the old tyrant in uniform, in charge of the landing-stage, who at ordinary times was prompt to chase us from the pontoon, now beamed benignantly and lent a hand to get us up the ship's side. We were the heroes of the moment, and knew well that the dozen or so boys on the quay whose fathers were still at sea and who were curtly ordered to " Stand back, clear of that check ! " were green with envy.

On board, we were kept busy answering inquiries as to the welfare of friends and acquaintances, and had the unforgettable experience of hearing the crew singing their " homeward-bound " shanties, as they tramped round the capstan heaving the good ship into her berth. We tramped round with them with a sense of contentment too deep for words.

Stepney, in those days, was a grand place for a boy who wanted to be a sailor.

CHAPTER II

BLACKWALL PIER on a fine day seventy years ago, with a fresh westerly breeze and a three-quarter flood, was an attractive place for the lover of ships. It was the centre of a scene of packed maritime activity. Woolwich Reach at such a time would be crowded with sailing barges, ketches, schooners, and Goole " billiboys," with a Dutch galliot or two, and a smart, yacht-like fish-carrier, all on the move and tacking across the reach. On the Greenwich side a few light colliers would be boring their way through the flood, swinging the main topgallant sail.

Dodging about among the shipping were sure to be one or more of the quaint " penny steamers " of the day, with high funnels and chequered sides. The progress of such craft was accomplished by means of many shouts of " Easy ahead ! ", " Starn eas-ee ! ", " Stop her ! " sung out by the " bridge telegraph "— a ragged urchin who stood over the engine-room sky-light with his eye on the captain and interpreted each motion of the latter's hand to the engineer below.

In the foreground a weather-beaten homeward-bounder might be preparing to dock, looking very picturesque as she had come through without anchoring, her sea-going gear still aloft.

Ahead of her the tug kept a taut rope, just sufficient to make the flood leave a slight curl of water at her stem. With yards braced sharp up, sails neatly stowed,

21

flags streaming from the trucks, the glorious Red Ensign at her peak, and tacks and sheets still dangling from the clews of the courses, she presented a sight calculated to rouse the enthusiasm of even landlubbers, let alone romantic youth who gloried in tales of the sea.

And how inspiring was the appearance of the men— a score or so of swarthy, weather-beaten " hairy-breasters " in well-worn sea rig, with red or blue shirts tucked under a belt which carried a dagger-like sheath-knife, booted to the knee, heaving the best bower aboard and roaring out one of the shanties specially reserved for entering dock at the end of the voyage.

The manner in which the various craft in the river kept clear of one another was a mystery. Collisions that seemed inevitable were continually being avoided by a hair's breadth. It was the more remarkable as large ocean-going sailing-ships were being towed both up and down river, and only the very largest, such as the Yankee packet-ships from the London docks, had the safeguard of a second tug lashed alongside to stop their way in case of emergency.

Each vessel was in charge of an experienced water-man or pilot (large foreign-going ships had both, one at each end), and a wave of the hand from one navigator to another was sufficient, such was the perfection of the unwritten river code, to indicate the course the signaller intended to take.

Of course there were slight collisions, mere playful bumps which did no more harm than a brush of paint or tar would cure, and which indeed often helped the smaller craft on its way. The " Geordie " brigs were said to be adepts in this nice point of practical seaman-ship. They had the art, it was believed, of bumping their larger neighbours at just the correct angle to help them round on to a new tack, when it was necessary to go about.

Nor must the " dumb barges " be omitted. They had no propelling power save the tide, on which they lazily drifted, broadside on, in midstream. The solitary lighterman who composed the crew usually stood with arms akimbo in the head, " monarch of all he surveyed." Everything else had to give way to him, and he knew it. Nevertheless, when some exasperated waterman, having to make a tack or otherwise inconvenience himself on account of " the lord of the river," gave vent to his feelings in heated language, the grinning bargee would so far unbend as to perform a double shuffle on the scuttle hatch.

Now and again, however, it happened that some pugnacious north-countryman would decline to give way and, with a gentle tap on the quarter, would push the heavy lighter out of the orthodox 'thwart the tide position. Then indeed his wrath was aroused, and the man who tended the cork fender to ease the blow would be entertained to a flow of Billingsgate as blue as the deep sea. . . .

Besides the panorama on the river, there was the motley crowd on the pier—full of interest for the student of humanity. Close to the dock entrance was the famous, or infamous, " tap-house," where much liquor was consumed every flood tide, when the " craft " and shipping were being docked and undocked. Jack, outward bound and attended with female friends, lingered here, until forced to take the " pier-head-jump," when his ship was lying " on the knuckle " and the tow-rope was being passed to the waiting tug-boat.

Inside the long narrow tap-room a fiddle or two scraped to keep the hilarity going to the last. The ladies here were not often parting from husbands; nevertheless, they were on the most affectionate terms with their partners. Free fights with one another alternated with hugging, kissing, blessings and cursings. Indeed for an hour or two the scene rivalled anything to be seen at the notorious " Paddy's Goose " in the Highway at its rowdiest.

Then the boarding-house runners, usually athletic six-footers, roughly shepherded their charges on to the pierhead, to make sure of their embarkation and see their " advance notes " were not invalidated. They literally threw the more refractory ones on board, and had to keep close watch to see some of them did not tumble ashore again.

Even then they were sometimes evaded or brushed aside. Venus—the Ratcliff Highway variety—flushed and boisterous on the quay, was more often than not the cause of the trouble. Her cheery endearments, intended to speed the parting guest, acted contrariwise : though the interested spectator might observe she was casting anxious glances toward the homeward-bound ship, sheering alongside at the upper end of the pier. " Off with the old love and on with the new " was the Highway philosophy; simply expressed in the ancient formula : " Get up, Jack, and let John sit down."

Ships undocking on the flood were taken into the river stern foremost. As the tide caught a vessel's quarter she was allowed to drift upstream and was checked on the knuckle of the landing-stage. She was followed all the way by a confused crowd of friends giving and receiving hasty farewells. Messages loving and reproachful, prayers for good luck and defiant wishes for the reverse, were mixed with facetious requests to " Bring me home a monkey, Bill," or " 'Ware those Melbourne wenches, Jack "; all to be cut short by a stentorian shout : " Stand clear the checks there ! " Then a general scamper was made for safety and the rest of the " send off " was a medley of waving hats and yells.

As the vessel was dragged stern first from the lock there was a moment of anxiety for pilot and dockmaster. She had to be kept well to " windward " to clear the pier, yet checked before running too far into the tide-way, to enable the tug to pick up the tow-rope. The forecastle head was a scene of excitement and bustle; the pilot alternating orders to " Slack away ! " and " Hold on ! " while the men stood ready to pay out the great hempen hawser when the waterman in his boat had passed the heaving line to the tug.

A breathless minute, and the ship straightened up, head down river. The pilot blew his whistle, the rope settled on the bitts and the check-ropes were cast off. As the tug took the strain and the vessel sheered away from the quay, the boatswain looked round and gave the word : " Now, lads, give them ' good-bye ' ! "

The men sprang to the call. Some on the forecastle head, others half-way up the forerigging, made ready to wake the echoes with the time-honoured ritual of " the ringing cheers." With eyes on the leader and caps in hand, to be swung vigorously round the head in unison, they broke out into a thunderous " Hip, hip, hurrah ! " thrice repeated.

To the salute the crowd ashore replied, with equal heartiness, if with a little less force and unanimity. Those on board responded with yet another, and dispersed to their duties. The ceremony was finished.

How it affected others I cannot say, but for myself the cheers thrilled me through and through. Nowhere else have I heard such a full-throated burst of sound (unless it were when the Greenland fleet left Peterhead for the fishery) as when one of the regular Blackwall Indiamen was outward bound for the East. Those same " ringing cheers," I dare assert, have helped to win many a battle for the British.

The ship dwindled away down stream, and the folk slowly cleared off the pier. The blue flag, flown from the pier masthead during the period of flood, was hauled down. The lockgates were hove to, and " tide was over." Venus and the crimps departed to await Jack, homeward bound, at the dock entrance; those who had said " good-bye " in real earnest to make their way slowly homewards.

For the next ten or twelve hours Blackwall Pier would wear a deserted and forlorn appearance, and the broad river be left to coasters and barges sailing down on the ebb.

Does a flowing tide, I wonder, tend to raise one's spirits, and the ebb to depress them? I have often thought so. One suggests gaiety, the other gloom : is it not said of those about to die that their souls " go out with the ebb "?

CHAPTER III

BLACKWALL MEMORIES

MOST seamen have a favourite port, and Blackwall was my first and last love. Associations of half a lifetime are bound up with it.

There was a memorable Sunday afternoon in October, 1863, when I first saw that bonnie and once famous Glasgow clipper, the *Falcon*. She arrived in company with the *Flying Spur* and other crack clippers, British and American, and the neighbourhood turned out in force to welcome them. The ladies vied with each other in the elaborateness of their toilettes and the circumference of their crinolines, the enormous hoops of which it was an endless source of amusement to male juveniles to " squeeze up."

No less gay were the scenes when one of the famous Blackwallers, the old *Monarch* or *The Earl of Balcarres*—the last of the two-decker Indiamen—was leaving. Such ships carried fifty or sixty of a crew, without counting midshipmen and cuddy servants, and were manned chiefly by local mariners. Half the parish would be on the pier to see them off. The Highway element was not much in evidence on such occasions, and the wives, sisters and sweethearts of the departing made a pleasant and comely picture.

Once, when Green's *Barham* was leaving, I noticed an elderly couple seeing their son off. The mother had drawn attention to herself by the unlimited and

27

impossible advice she was giving her son, who received it lightheartedly, with mysterious rejoinders about a " cat."

Then the ship sheered away from the quay. Springing to the rail, the boy drew a kitten from his jacket and waved it round his head hilariously, while the cat gave vent to vigorous " meeows." The indignant old lady turned to her husband: " The wretch has stolen the . . ." she began. But her remarks were lost in a roar of laughter from the onlookers which lasted till the " cheers " were given, and the great ship dropped gaily down the river.

Sailors and their folk made no great fuss over parting. It was different with emigrants. The latter were embarked in dock; and groups of men, women and children, miserably huddled together among boxes, chests and bundles, with tearful friends at their side, waited for hours on the quay when an emigrant ship for the Colonies was about to sail.

When I was very young I remember seeing two elderly women talking earnestly to a comely girl of about nineteen. " Dinna gang, lassie, dinna gang," they kept repeating. The girl never answered them, but with quivering lip and head held high, marched on board. So she sailed, leaving the two old souls weeping on the quay.

I expect it was a case of " following the lad." The ship was bound to New Zealand, and perhaps the bonnie lassie of '61 is now a grandmother herself and saw a grandchild of her own take his departure for " Flanders' fields."

Comedy sometimes turned to tragedy. When one of Wigram's Melbourne liners (the *Kent,* I think) was sailing, I saw one of the boatswain's mates spring into the forerigging to lead the cheering. He slipped and fell, striking his head against the fore channels and falling into the river, where he sank immediately.

The accident turned the glee of leave-taking to gloom at once. What made it more sad was that he was a young married man and the accident was witnessed by his wife on the quay, with her baby in her arms.

Besides emigrants, troops often embarked at Blackwall; and I have watched contingents of the disbanded soldiers of the East India Company disembarking there after the Indian Mutiny. They looked as if they had seen much service—bronzed and bearded veterans for the most part, in uniforms that had seen better days. Parties of them came home in Dunbar's ships, but there was mismanagement somewhere, for numbers of them landed penniless. In one case there was a general uproar and the pier tavern was wrecked. The soldiers were blamed, but local roughs were at the bottom of the mischief.

I saw one veteran, a fine-looking man, sitting on a bollard after the fray, covered with blood, his clothes torn from his back. The nature of his homecoming must have hurt him cruelly, for he was sobbing like a child. When he was spoken to he pointed to some scars on his chest, with a heart too full to reply. A thousand times, no doubt, in the heat and dust of Indian war he had looked forward to and pictured this homecoming. And this was the reality! I pitied him with all my heart.

There was an ugly side to Blackwall and the pier and it came out on occasions like this, or when a " hell-fire " ship was being supplied with a crew. I have seen a free fight and weapons used by crimps and seamen when the *Clymene*, a Liverpool ship, was sailing for India.

Poor Jack was very much at the mercy of these

land-sharks, the crimps. Occasionally, I am glad to say, the tables were turned. Some simple mariners from Aberdeen once " did " the wide-awake Highway runners in a delightful manner.

'Way back in the sixties the wool-clipper *Granite City* arrived in London from Aberdeen, where she had undergone extensive repairs, bringing with her a freight of granite kerb-stones. With this heavy cargo she was " well down in the pickle," and, as it was a dark, wintry night when she arrived, coming alongside Blackwall Pier she looked like a ship fully laden.

The crimps jumped to the conclusion she was from Sydney as usual, and the crowd of runners did not trouble to disabuse them. Arrangements were made for the men to put up at a certain boarding-house, (Paddy Finn's in Old Gravel Lane), and, pending the ship being berthed, the customary bottles of rum were passed aboard in generous profusion, together with certain small sums in cash asked for. Not being allowed to bring their cart on to the pier, the crimps waited for the men at the main dock entrance.

The canny Scots, however, were 'longshoremen, working the ship to London " by the run " on a lump sum basis, and their contract was finished as soon as the ship was through the locks. Being unencumbered with chests or kit, they left the dock, one at a time, by the pier entrance and made tracks for the night train for bonnie Scotland.

It meant death or disablement to mention the words *Granite City* for long after that in the Highway. But the incident was not allowed to be forgotten.

There was an ancient seller of preserved candy, whose pitch was just outside the dock entrance, who went by the name of " Blind Billy." He had been a boatswain in the Blackwallers, and he possessed the gift of coining appropriate phrases for any unusual or

lubberly happening which took place in his neighbourhood, which he retailed to all and sundry in a
voice like a foghorn.

"Blind Billy" seized on the incident of the
Granite City, and discussed it with "damnable itera-
tion" with the old Irish applewomen who sat near
him, whenever the runners were about. And much as
they disliked it they were powerless to prevent him.

Speaking of the applewomen reminds me of an
Irish colony which flourished behind Robin Hood
Lane. It was a thriving colony if noise counted for
anything, but no one, unless they were "one of
ours," ventured to explore it. Even the police, when
the fun within grew fast and furious and the cry of
"Murder!" resounded, dared not enter singly, but
awaited reinforcements. The residents of the adjoin-
ing respectable Cotton Street were often awakened at
"the murk midnight hour" by the wailing and
screeching that issued from "Cut-throat Alley." I do
not suppose anyone was often "kilt," though there
was doubtless many an "illigant bating," but woe
betide the stranger who sought to interfere within their
gates.

In truth, Blackwall was a place of many thrills. It
was a rendezvous for those who loved to see "the
stately ships sail out," and it was a place also of much
poverty and hardship. In any case the stream of life
ran colourfully there.

CHAPTER IV

LONDON RIVER

AFTER a boyhood spent in Stepney, with occasional trips to Peterhead and Aberdeen, it was from Blackwall I sailed on my first long voyage to the southward in the *Chaa-sze,* a ship of about six hundred tons register, bound to Sydney, N.S.W. I remember how indignant I was when a friend asked me if I was not afraid to venture so far in so small a ship. At the time such a question appeared absurd, but I confess I modified my opinion somewhat when, two months later, we were rolling the easting down in fifty degrees of south latitude, with decks full of water.

It was to Blackwall we returned at the end of that voyage, and it was at Blackwall a few years later that, as mate of the *Norman Court,* I had the satisfaction, as we dropped alongside the famous pier, of being told by one of the dock officials who had known me from childhood that we had made the best passage of the season from China with teas.

It was at Blackwall again, in 1874, as master of the same clipper, when we docked on a dark autumn night, that I enjoyed one of the supreme moments of my career—that of being hailed by Captain Stevens, the dockmaster, with the news that we had beaten our great antagonist on that passage, the celebrated *Sir Lancelot,* from whom we had parted company in the China seas. " A feather in your cap, my boy," he shouted cheerily, and so, in truth, I felt it.

I was always delighted when I heard that we were booked for the Blackwall Dock, or " the East," as it was more generally called. Every nook and corner of it was familiar to me, and to be sent to one of the upper docks at once took away half the pleasure of getting home.

This satisfaction, experienced as a youngster, remained when I became mate, if only for the fact that one was not required to rig in the jib-boom or cockbill the lower yards here, as was the case at the London and St. Catherine's Docks.

This was no small matter in the case of the *Norman Court* with her heavy spars, the boom being especially awkward to handle.

It could prove awkward, too. On one occasion at West Quay, ahead of where we were to berth, was a large Liverpool ship, with a tall flagstaff projecting from her taffrail. The people on board had been requested to remove this, but declined.

As we were being thrust in, broadside on, by the tugs, I saw the ancient transport foreman chuckling to himself and heard him say, " Here's a lady with a ' horn ' will make that Liverpool man fly round." And sure enough it did. Our raking boom glided across his taffrail and was about to strike his colours and sweep his poop for him, when a rotund officer and brassbound apprentice tore along the deck and with frantic speed unshipped the spar in the nick of time.

The " mud-pilot "—he who boarded the ship at Gravesend—often objected to take us up to dock without the boom being rigged in, as well as with the precaution of a second tug lashed alongside.

In 1872 after making the passage from China, Macao to Gravesend against the monsoon, in ninety-three days, the tugs came up one stormy afternoon

C

too late for us to dock on the day tide. As soon as
the cable was shackled on I sent the crew below and
set an anchor watch. The pilot, an elderly man and
a stranger to me, acquiesced :

" That's right, Mr. Mate; we'll rig the boom in as
we tow up to-morrow."

At supper-time I suggested letting it stand, but he
was more than dubious and declined to compromise,
though I raised no demur to his suggestion of a second
tug. However, I treated him well, and being exhilar-
ated with an excellent meal and other creature comforts,
he at length agreed to forego his request about the
boom.

As we approached the dock next morning I could
see he was not altogether easy. However, we reached
the pier without mishap and tied up alongside the
landing-stage to await the exit of one or two outward-
bounders.

The pilot was much relieved. He came up to me
smiling :

" Well, Mr. Mate, here we are, and the boom
all right. I think I *will* have that drop of rum you
spoke about."

" Why, of course. . . . Steward ! "

But the steward was in the act of filling the glasses
when there was an uproar on deck and the dockmaster's
stentorian shout :

" *Norman Court* ahoy ! Slack away your head
rope, and be lively about it ! This ship'll have that
—— long boom out of you ! "

" Oh lord ! oh lord ! " said the still unrefreshed
pilot, " why didn't I rig it in ? "

However, the waterman had sprung to the rescue,
and the outward-bounder, a lumbering, deep-draughted
ship, cleared us by inches. Nor, though the danger
was past, could I persuade the old pilot to take his

grog until the ship was in the locks and he had given up charge.

On the next homecoming of the *Norman Court*, my first voyage as master, we had another trifling mishap at Blackwall Pier.

It was a bitter winter's morning when we got the mud-pilot at Gravesend, and, there being time to save the tide at Blackwall, he kept going.

He made no demur about the jib-boom and we arrived off the entrance to the East India Dock shortly after daybreak, when the operation of swinging the ship to the flood commenced.

Now the *Norman Court* was a cockle-shell behind the tug, which happened on that occasion to be the famed *Sir Robert Bruce*. The latter was the most powerful tug on the river, and was chiefly employed in dragging up the great timber-laden ships from Quebec, which drew twenty feet of water and more. She only took us in consideration of extra remuneration.

Her skipper employed the same tactics with us as he would have done with a timber drogher of a couple of thousand tons. Instead of sailing us round, he tried to turn us as on a pivot. The pilot was forward, but Bill White, our regular waterman, was at the wheel and roared out to him to have a care what he was doing.

He did not seem to see it, and got the rope to a sharp angle abaft the beam. To a timber drogher this would not have mattered, but to a fine-lined yacht like the *Norman Court*, which would move astern as fast as she would ahead, the case was quite the reverse.

As soon as she felt the strain on the rope she began to slip astern over to the Blackwall side and, before the pilot could realize what had happened and let go an anchor, had cannoned into the landing-stage with her port quarter, and bounced off, head up river. She struck the landing-stage with so much force that the mooring chains, flashing fire, gave way, and the whole contraption broke adrift and started on a trip of its own up river, the landing-stage officials and some other people still upon it.

It was all done in a moment. I saw the old fogey in charge of the landing-stage, his blue coat tails streaming behind him, rush as he thought for safety, then, at the widening gulf, pause irresolutely. A vision of the same old martinet when, in my boyhood days, he had chased us remorselessly from the precincts of the stage rushed into my mind, and I laughed.

It was undignified perhaps and I greatly fear he saw me, but the temptation was too great, and I laughed.

No bodily mischief, of course, was done. The ship herself was little the worse for the impact—one of the mooring posts made a slight bruise on her counter. The pontoon suffered more and had to go into dry dock to be re-caulked. The dock company put in a claim for damages, but Baring Brothers laughed at them. The pilot, however, felt guilty and did not claim his pilotage, though on my next return home the matter was settled.

At that time, I believe, a ship hailing from the port of London was not compelled to take a Thames pilot, and Trinity House in consequence were not liable for damages, unless to a very limited extent. But ships hailing from Aberdeen, Liverpool and other places were so compelled, and damages arising from the pilot's negligence could be recovered.

For this reason some London shipowners, whose ships sailed regularly from the Thames, altered their port of registry to Aberdeen and elsewhere.

While I was in her, the *Norman Court* always

THE "SCOTTISH MAID."
Built by Hall's of Aberdeen in 1839.

Facing p. 36

docked at Blackwall; but by 1880 the glory attending racing with the teas from China was over. The Blackwall passenger frigates were also fast disappearing, and with them went the romantic attraction of Blackwall Pier.

My last time of docking at Blackwall in the ship was early in 1879, at the close of one of the hardest winters of modern times. We had to beat every inch of the way up Channel, the wind never varying more than a point in our favour.

We came in sight of the Scillies on January 19th, on our forty-second day out from Capetown, and encountered a strong easterly wind as soon as we got into the chops of the Channel. That day we made our first tack, and thereafter, hot and strong, we caught it.

With Scilly bearing north-north-west we went away to the southward under reefed topsails and reefed foresail. For the next four or five days, never carrying more, and sometimes only able to show lower topsails, we hammered away against a very heavy head sea and shipped nasty lumps of water persistently.

On January 23rd when, according to dead reckoning—observation being impossible—we should have been off the Start, we were still off the Wolf lighthouse. We were not aware then that the easterly wind had already lasted a number of weeks and caused a strong westerly current, running, as we afterwards discovered, at about a knot an hour.

Then the wind moderated a little, though it still held a dead muzzler, and, standing in under reefed topsails, we were by the following Sunday in smoother water under the lee of the Start. We fell in here with a fleet of Salcombe fishermen who, the weather being thick, gave me the correct bearing of the Point and, in reply to my inquiry as to how long the easterly

wind had lasted, bawled feelingly through the fog:
" Six sanguinary weeks ! "

On January 28th we tacked off the Bill of Portland,
and the following night tacked again with the light on
the Digue at Cherbourg bearing due south.

The next day we tacked with St. Catherine's
bearing north by east, and I see that I made the hopeful
entry in the log : " Getting on."

By this time we were carrying topgallant sails
again, the royal yards having been sent down off the
Wolf, and on the 30th sighted the Owers Light and
went about.

Next morning, some time before noon, we fetched
in under Beachy Head, and to our relief, everyone
being dead tired of continual " Main topsail haul-O ! "
sighted a London tug-boat, the *Scotia*.

The tug bore down on us and ranged up under
our quarter. The figure he asked to tow us up to
London almost took my breath away. I offered him
£50, at which a " loud laugh laughed he," and made
as though to leave us. I, too, tacked to the southward
again, at which the merry one modified his first demand
a little.

Still no arrangement was come to. The mainsail
was still hanging in the gear and all hands were
listening anxiously to our conversation. I gave the
order to " set the mainsail ! " and the men literally and
audibly groaned as they boarded the tack and hauled
aft the sheet.

Before the operation was complete the tugmaster
thought again, and to everyone's satisfaction, mine as
much as the men, sang out : " Haul that mainsail up,
and give us your rope."

The words acted like magic. That sail was at the
yard in a moment, and I have never seen the rest of
the canvas come in more quickly than it did then.

Fear that the hard bargainer might repent spurred the men on to beat all previous records.

On our arrival in the Thames we found that, with only one exception, the Australian wool-clippers, anxious to save the February sales, had put into Falmouth or Plymouth. Tugs had been sent from London to tow them up, at little more cost than we paid from Beachy. The sole exception was the splendid 1,500-ton iron clipper, the *Mermerus*; she and the *Norman Court* were the only two to keep the seas, though, had I known the circumstances, the *Mermerus* would have had that honour to herself.

We were all dead beat with our bitter cold experience in the Channel. Fortunately I had a cask of " Cape smoke " on board, and a tot of this occasionally served to cheer the men up, besides making fine hot punch for the after guard.

On entering the river we noticed that most of the iron tugs, lighters, etc., had much of their paint rubbed off and were very rusty about the waterline. On inquiry we learnt that this was owing to the floating ice that encumbered the Thames, and that during the previous month some of the docks had been frozen over and even the river itself above the bridge.

That was the last time I docked at Blackwall, and never, I may say, was the sight of the historic pier so welcome.

CHAPTER V

AN OLD-TIME LONDON SHIPOWNER

NEARLY everyone nowadays knows that the famous *Cutty Sark* was built to the order of Messrs John Willis & Son, the once-renowned London shipowners. Fewer people, perhaps, are aware that the founder of the firm was not the John Willis who was such a well-known figure about Blackwall in the eighties of last century and whose " white hat " has since become famous, but one who reigned a generation before him, to wit, his father.

John Willis the elder was a familiar figure of my boyhood. My father served him for many years and heard much of the story of his early life over a glass of grog in the cuddies of the clippers *Merse* and *Lammermuir*. I give these few reminiscences as I heard them from my father, with the addition of some of my own recollections of the old gentleman. They are characteristic of a man who, starting his career with little more than the clothes he stood up in, ended it some sixty years later with a considerable fortune accumulated by means of dogged perseverance, integrity and tenacity of purpose.

John Willis the elder was a native of the small fisher-port of Eyemouth in Berwickshire. He was born about the year 1788, and his parents were people of very modest means who were only able to endow their son with an iron constitution and an indomitable will, and but little else.   John's father died while he was still very young and left him in charge of an uncle as guardian. The village school supplied him with a working knowledge of " the three R's."

Guardian and ward did not view matters in the same light, and it happened one day when young John was about thirteen years old, that a violent altercation arose between them.   Hard words on the uncle's part were followed by blows; the lad retaliated with the weapon nearest to hand, namely a brick; and, as he himself told my father, the last he saw of his natural guardian was on the floor, laid out flat, the result of a well-aimed missile.

Thus John Willis left home.   At first, I believe he joined a small coasting craft, but a year or two later was serving in a West Indiaman sailing out of London.

One voyage the ship he was in was berthed in the newly-made West India Dock at Limehouse.   This dock had been excavated from a marsh, and its approaches were in a very miry condition.   The ship captains and others who did business at the dock used an ancient hostelry close by known as " The Blue Posts."   They were invariably in a hurry and invariably in a mess, and the " Boots " at the inn did a roaring business attending to their needs.   To this " Boots," in his leisure hours of an evening, John Willis became assistant; and did so well that in a short time he had accumulated a pocket fortune of several pounds.

Casting about in his mind for an investment for this sum, he remembered the fiddling and banjo-playing propensities of the plantation darkies in the West Indies, and sank his small capital in fiddle strings. These found such a good market on the ensuing voyage that Willis went on to other and more ambitious commodities.   In this way he laid the foundations of his after success.   Voyage after voyage his profits increased; he became second and chief mate and finally captain, attaining command of a West Indiaman at a remarkably early age.

That sterling worth lay behind his good fortune, and was probably the cause of it, is evidenced by a story which has been put on record by one of his grand-children, Mr. James Kirkaldy.

That gentleman wrote that when John Willis was mate his ship went ashore one voyage coming up Channel. " The captain and crew abandoned the vessel, but my grandfather remained on board and prevented plundering. He sent word to the owners, the weather moderated and the cargo was saved. He was given command, and invested in the ship the money given him by the underwriters."

He married early and had a large family, six sons and four daughters. The eldest boy, " Young John," as he was called when I first knew him, in distinction to his father " Old John," was the after owner of the *Cutty Sark*.

During his active seafaring career the elder Willis lived near Wapping, and was much respected by the other members of the flourishing Scottish community in the neighbourhood. The national rallying point was a famous local hostelry, known as the " Wha dare meddle wi' me," though its sign was merely the " Scots' Arms " and its emblem a huge thistle. It was kept by one " Luckie " Wood.

A Wapping resident who was a close friend of John Willis's from his earliest days was George Yates, who kept a grocer's shop and did much business with the small Scottish vessels trading from the north-east coast.

Yates had a famous manager of whom it was said that he never left the shop, except to go to bed, for thirty years. His name was Henry Aston, and he afterwards built up a considerable fortune, becoming a shipowner and having a part share in the tea-clipper *Chinaman*. His wealth was acquired mainly by providing foreign-going shipmasters with provisions, such as cheeses, hams, etc., to sell abroad on half-shares. He also was a Scotsman, his native place being somewhere about the Moray Firth.

These and a few others were the cronies of John Willis. The little grocery shop with the large cellars was the rendezvous for most of the seafarers hailing from north of Aberdeen. Often, as a boy, I have waited outside the parlour door sucking a piece of candy, while within old John, Yates, my father and others fought their battles over again.

This sanctum was not free to all comers. The company was select and restricted to those " up in the stirrups." Old John Brodie who had Brodie's ship-repairing dock at Rotherhithe; Captain Pirie, shipowner and shipbuilder, who built the *Whiteadder, Red Riding Hood, Argonaut, Borealis* and several fast ships for the Adelaide trade; Ross the ballastman, and McLachlan, the nautical instrument maker, whose business premises were in Great Hermitage Street—these were the senior members of the Scottish clan and the privileged guests in the parlour.

In those days most tradesmen lived over their shops, the migration to Bow and Hackney not yet having set in, and many were the jovial little supper-parties where owners, shipmasters and tradesmen sat down convivially together on terms of equality.

Though the snuggery was select, each and every scion of the breed was welcomed in the shop and enter-tained in a more lowly manner by honest Henry Aston. The latter kept a sort of register, mainly mental, I believe, of all trustworthy men looking for berths, the chief qualification being that they were Scotch. Thus if a man came to John Willis with a recommendation from Aston, no questions were asked and no test required. But all owners were not so easily satisfied, and with a few the dour Scottish sectarianism was the deciding factor.

This was not the case with the old sea-dog Willis. In this matter he copied the famous Duchess of Gordon, who, irritated by a lady recommending a cook through laying overmuch emphasis on the orthodoxy of her religious views, " cut short the cackle " by exclaiming : " Damn her religion ! Can she make good minced collops ? "

I do not mean to say there were many shipowners who would reject a good seaman even if he followed Mahomet ; but with one of them at least, old James Anderson, a native of Peterhead, it was a *sine qua non* that all young applicants from the north should have attended the ministrations of a " Free Kirk " minister. Old James had covenanting blood in his veins ; he had a relative who was minister of the Free Kirk at Peterhead, and when any young member of the latter's flock decided to sail to the southward he was sent to the " Chief " in London.

Anderson's " ship's husband "—marine superintendent, he would be called nowadays—became very disgruntled at having to give preference to these raw recruits from the north. He adopted a sarcastic formula with which he greeted all fresh applicants :

" Where are you from ? "

" Peterhead."

" Ah ! d'you belong to the Free Kirk there ? "

" Aye."

" All right : trouble yourself no further ; your fortune's made."

But old John Willis preferred to encourage those who, like himself, had " come on board through the hawse pipe." More than one of his successful shipmasters, of whom Stuart of the " Tweed " was one, and my father another, owed the advance in their fortunes to the fact that, as mates of Peterhead brigs or the smart little schooners that carried mails and passengers from Wapping to the northern burgh, they had been used to go to old George Yates's shop for the scanty stores.

Old John Willis was the hero, it has always been my conviction, of the fine old shanty " Stormalong." The original version of the song is too long to quote, but there are points about it which indicate that " Stormalong " was none other than old John Willis; " old Stormy's son " being John Willis the younger, and " the ship he built " the famous *Cutty Sark*.

Certain it is that old John was a seaman of the old school, fearless and beloved as was his antitype, and of the daring go-ahead disposition that gave old " Stormalong " his cognomen. One voyage, at least, which he made, was solely due to his " stormalong " proclivities.

One winter, I think it was that of the year 1835, there was a furious succession of westerly winds and gales. When John Willis, then a sea-captain, ran down before the wind from Gravesend, bound to Demerara, the Downs were crowded with shipping, all lying wind-bound.

John cleared the Prince's Channel with the wind a dead muzzler, but slightly moderating. Instead of running through the Gull Stream, he turned the ship's head for the North Goodwin and stood to the southward for the French coast. Then, with a reef in his topsails, he beat to the westward by the back of the Goodwins and so got into the Channel.

By a stroke of luck the wind now backed southerly, though it was piping again. However, the ship's head was at last pointing down Channel, and under all the canvas she could carry, old John stormed along.

Driving her for all she was worth, next morning he scraped past St. Catherine's.

The southerly wind having come away during the night, the ships in the Downs hesitated to get under way. Only a few did so, when, the wind veering again to the west, they once more had to let go the anchor.

Willis, however, by this time was nearing Portland Bill and getting sea-room. Driving her hard, he weathered Ushant and, experiencing a slant of luck in the Bay, fetched down to the north-east trades. These were brisk, and he made a fair passage to Demerara.

The port was short of shipping, merchants were anxious to send their sugar and rum to London, and Willis speedily loaded his ship at a high rate of freight. He was soon rolling back before the westerly gales which were still holding his competitors wind-bound in the Downs.

He assured my father that when he arrived back several of the West Indian fleet that he had passed when outward bound were still at anchor in the Downs, while others were sheltering in various ports down Channel.

Old John had followed the course taken by probably the most powerful type of merchant vessel then afloat, the packet-ships which carried mails and passengers between New York and London. There were no steam tugs at that time to tow ships " fair wind or foul " to Beachy Head, yet the packets never, except under the most extraordinary circumstances, brought up in the Downs to wait for a fair wind, as did the ordinary merchant vessel and Indiaman.

Furnished with double crews and pilots noted for their ability and daring, these ships were thrashed to the westward at the back of the Goodwins, blow high or blow low, though they might be reduced to double-reefed topsails doing it. So they carried on down Channel, and were on a wind, perhaps, for the greater part of the trip across the Western Ocean.

A passage of forty days was not considered anything out of the ordinary for a packet-ship bound to the westward during the winter season. But for the most part their runs were made in much better time than this and afford examples of extraordinary resource and endurance on the part of captains and officers. Their large and unruly crews were kept busy reefing and furling as the gales increased; or " piling the muslin " on to the hard-driven ship when the wind abated in the least degree. He was no weakling who had served his time as mate or boatswain in a New York packet-ship.

And old John in a " built-by-the-mile-and-cut-off-by-the-fathom " West Indiaman had beat his way out along the road of these, the finest ships afloat. He had not earned the name of " Old Stormalong " for light reasons.

I remember another instance of his " stamp-and-go " methods when he was getting on in years.

In 1850 his eldest son took command of the latest addition to the Willis's fleet. This was the *St. Abbs*, built especially for the China trade and a fine ship for her day, though a long way from being a *Cutty Sark*.

On the homeward passage young John had fallen sick and, encountering head winds in the Channel, sought shelter inside the " Wight." Old John, when he heard of it, was furious at the delay, and in his own impetuous fashion posted at once to Portsmouth.

Much to his son's disgust he turned up on board. He demanded to be told the reason " why the ship had put in there? ", " why she was wasting time? " etc., and much more to the same effect. He ended by packing his son off home, announcing his determination to " take the ship to the Downs myself."

Before the poor skipper was over the side the crew

were purchasing the anchor, and, in spite of local warnings as to bad weather brewing, the *St. Abbs* put to sea.

As foretold, the wind flew into the south-south-east and increased rapidly. Old John would not put back, but scorning the suggestions of his mates, hung on to his sail till it looked as though the topmasts would go over the side.

Hour by hour the weather thickened and those on board lost their bearings. Then at last old Willis reefed down.

He was only just in time. Through the thick blanket of mist they suddenly discovered themselves perilously close to Beachy Head and on a dead lee shore.

The ship was under too low sail to come round in stays, and too close to the land to wear. The only thing to do was to stand on, carrying all the canvas she would stand up under, and trust to Providence to weather the Head and the Royal Sovereign Shoal.

They did so, and providence favoured them, as it often does men of old John's type. While it was still touch and go with them the wind southed a point or more and they scraped past the land safely.

The men had fairly made up their minds that they would have to swim for it, and when they had safely weathered the Head they were loud in their denunciations of what they called " Old Stormy's " pigheadedness.

Yet it must not be assumed that old John was in the habit of taking foolish risks. Had he done so he would hardly have come safely through about thirty years as master of a class of vessel so notoriously unwieldy as the West Indiamen of his day.

Many of that class of ships were of almost rectangular construction, so built that the sugar hogsheads might stow well. They were so sluggish and clumsy, and withal so slow, that it was said they could push a floating cocoanut ahead for miles, and carry a bunch of bananas from Port Royal to the Downs in the dead water under the vessel's lee quarter. One of them, the *Spheroid*, achieved fame by carrying away her topmasts when she was driven up to the speed of six knots.

By 1853 John Willis had a fleet of at least four ships—the *John Willis, Borderer, St. Abbs* and *Janet Willis*. In that year my father arrived in London in a Glasgow barque, the *Niagara*. He took service with old John and was appointed master of the *Merse* of seven hundred tons, then on the stocks at Sunderland.

As old Willis often asserted, he " never gave an order for a new ship until he was able to pay for her," so he must have been by this time a man of considerable substance. He would not allow any of his captains to have a share in their ships, and avoided all entangling alliances with shipbrokers, merchants and tradesmen.

In this last respect he differed from most London shipowners. Green's, for instance, were shipbuilders and brokers as well as shipowners, and Duncan Dunbar had a large export liquor trade. Dunbar at this time was the largest London shipowner; just after the Crimean War and the Mutiny he cannot have owned less than fifty ships. In 1858, at one time, I counted eight large vessels, all flying his house flag, at the loading berths in the East India Export Dock. His ships, with the notable exceptions of the ill-fated *Dunbar* and the magnificent *Duncan Dunbar*, were patriotically named after famous British victories, *Albuera, Talavera, Vimiera, Salamanca*, and the like.

Willis's ships were mostly named from prominent

D

features of his native Berwickshire. The notable exception was the *Cutty Sark*, but that scantily attired damsel immortalized by Burns may be presumed to have been a Berwickshire lassie.

Whenever possible old Willis met his ships at Gravesend, bundled the skipper ashore to enter his ship and greet his family, and took charge himself. He almost lived on board whilst the ship was in London.

When I first remember him, his home was in Clapton Square, near old Hackney Church. He had removed there, far from the smell of pitch and tar, at the instigation of his daughters, it was said. Nevertheless, when one of his ships was in London, he seldom failed to be on board by 8.30 in the morning.

It was the hour when the apprentices and others were supposed to return from breakfast, and the old man was not altogether displeased, I fancy, when they turned up late. It gave him an opportunity for comparing their lack of energy with his own punctuality, and usually ended with a gruff: " Ye lazy loons ! ye've had fish for breakfast, I suppose," the point of the joke being that much time would be wasted picking their teeth after breakfasting on a " New Gravel Lane bullock, fifty ribs a side "—in other words, a red herring.

The journey from his home to the ship took him an hour, and he always called at a little shop near the dock for his daily allowance of snuff, one pennyworth, carefully screwed up in paper and kept in his waistcoat pocket. Old John was not parsimonious, but snuff-boxes he thought frivolous.

Though he left home so early he always had a full breakfast before leaving. He insisted on porridge and gave his cook more trouble than she cared for to prepare it. But old John was not to be denied, and the lady had " to like it or leave it " as the East End saying has it.

If " the girls " overslept themselves old John roused " all hands " in much the same way as he would have turned out a refractory watch at sea. His wife and daughters had to rouse out and bear a hand likewise. For a short time there was pandemonium below stairs. More than once the staff got a moment's notice to " bundle and go," and Mrs. Willis had to prepare the " stirabout " herself.

The two eldest sons, John and Robert, at this time did most of the City business, and the old man had the ships to himself. He could not bear to be long away from them, especially from his beloved *Lammermuir*. When a ship had to be re-coppered she was taken to the dockyard at Rotherhithe, owned by an old friend, Captain Pirie, of Messrs. Bilbe & Pirie, and the old gentleman invariably made the trip by water himself.

The dry dock was some distance from Blackwall, and on one memorable occasion I was allowed to make the cruise. It was at the time the " Great Eastern " was being launched from Messrs. Scott, Russell & Company's yard on the Isle of Dogs. She took the water broadside on, but I cannot say that I " saw the launch," for it took about three weeks, but I saw some of it, and the ship certainly looked a monster in comparison with the other craft.

In the dry dock old Willis saw that great attention was paid to the weighing out of the old copper sheathing, while the apprentices were kept busy with a bucket apiece, picking up the old nails and scraps of yellow metal as the shipwrights worked away on the stages.

It was glorious fun for my brother and myself.

Old Willis cruised about, keeping a keen eye on the men at work and occasionally watching us at our games. He had one stock question for all boys— "What are ye going to be, a sodger or a sailor?" I fancy he considered all other occupations merely superfluous.

It was not always plain sailing. Once we trundled the wheel of a handbarrow over his gouty toe and fairly withered under his wrath, expressed in good deep-sea terms. The mate was summoned at once and instructed to see "the little devils" over the gangway —"more sharper."

Or it might be "ballast heaving" that we watched. The ballast heavers were mostly Irishmen, and, nearly naked, the poor fellows laboured hard for little money. The "big shilling" (half a crown) was then a dock labourer's daily wage, working from nine to four, with twenty minutes' spell for "Beer-oh" at noon.

After the labours of the day these men were compelled to adjourn to certain beer-houses to receive their wage. These beer-houses were kept or owned by their employers, and it was a common practice for some excuse or other to be trumped up to cause delay, so that the tired men might be glad to sit down and drink beer—to the good of the house and the detriment of their own families.

I regret to have to record that Willis's friend, the ballastman, though a dour Scottish Presbyterian, owned two beer-shops, one at Blackwall and one at Wapping, handy for whichever dock his men might be working in.

All of John Willis's sons were brought up in the good old fashion—"in the fear of God and a rope's end." Four of them at one time or another commanded ships belonging to their father; and of

the four the best known and the most successful was
the eldest, John.

The latter, though a shrewd business man, did not
follow the primitive methods of his father. As the
saying goes, " his father had been born before him,"
and young John was able to start where old John left
off. He was not above taking a rise out of the old
gentleman when increasing years had worn thin the
latter's patience.

On one occasion he neglected to relieve his father
on board the *Lammermuir*. Old John had important
business to transact and, as the minutes slipped by,
he waited with growing impatience. There was no
earthly reason why he should not have departed, but
the *Lammermuir* was the apple of his eye and not to be
left lightly.

When at last the culprit arrived he was received
with great sternness. Old John finished up a lengthy
tirade by protesting that he had been forced to stay
by the ship for hours, kicking his heels. His son
carelessly whistled the refrain of a popular ditty in
which a milkmaid answers her gallant :

> " ' There was nobody asked you,
>   Sir,' she said,"

and turning round as he left the cuddy, made a polite
bow and repeated emphatically :

> " ' Nobody asked you,
>   Sir,' she said."

Old John had no weapon handy with which to
counter an attack of this kind, and age was telling. He
contented himself by turning to my father :

" What dae ye think o' the damned idjits, Shewan ?
They're a' ganging gyte. . . . Tell the steward to
put the grog on the table." It was a mild conclusion
for the old warrior.

Old John, of course, was no teetotaller. Few seamen were in those days. A temperate man was accustomed to a tot of rum in the morning coffee—coffee royal. Then when the sun was " over the fore-yard," that is, towards noon, another libation was poured. At sea in hot weather " sangoree " was customary for this ceremony. It was composed of best Demerara rum, qualified with the juice of fresh limes and sweetened with sugar. This was a drink for the gods; even with ordinary lime-juice the drink was " mighty enticin'."

In my boyhood days many of the West Indiamen served out rum three times a day, though in the Black-wall East Indiamen the allowance was one gill only, served out at noon. In those ships, when the chief officer had taken the sun and found it noon, he notified the fact by ordering the boatswain to

> " Heave the log,
> Pipe to grog,
> And strike the bell eight."

A year or two before I went to sea the Board of Trade insisted on lime-juice, slightly fortified with rum, being served out daily to all seamen in foreign-going British ships. The ration of rum had in consequence been reduced, though the more liberal shipowners still put two or three quarter casks of sound Demerara on board their ships, to afford a glass of grog to the crew on dirty nights at sea.

In my first ship, the *Chaa-sze*, each watch had a bottle of rum sent along each Saturday night and Sunday at noon. When all hands were called a tot of rum was always served out, as well as on nights when the weather was very dirty.

In my next ship, the *Reigate* (1863), grog was served out only when all hands were called; and in

"LAMMERMUIR."
John Willis' favourite ship.

the *Black Prince* (1866) not a drop was served at sea, only when working cargo in port.

By 1880 most British ships were dry; a small quantity of brandy only was carried as "medical comforts." But one had to be almost at death's door before any "comfort" was vouchsafed.

By the year 1856 British shipowners were waking up to the fact that there was much room for improvement, as well in the modelling of their ships as in their rigging and sail plans. Wire rope for shrouds and stays was displacing the less enduring and more clumsy hemp. Hand-reefing topsails were giving place to the so-called "self-reefing" variety—Cunningham's patent. The great advantage of these was that they could be reefed from the deck by means of double halyards fitted in such a manner that on lowering one of them the topsail yard was made to revolve and roll the sail round it. Patent capstan windlasses had not yet come into use, but were not to be long delayed. The *Chaa-sze* was one of the first ships to be fitted with one of them in 1860.

Many old shellbacks despised these new-fangled methods and could not be induced to see good in any of them. They preferred ships where reefing topsails meant "a labour of love," to speak sarcastically, and would rather lay out on a topsail yard for hours securing the close reef than do the same thing from the deck by a few minutes' work at the reefing halyards, with a shanty to help them.

Nevertheless, patent topsails had certain disadvantages. They were fitted with a sliding apron, controlled by iron slats in the middle of the sail. This "blacksmith's shop," as it was called, was confoundedly heavy and frequently resulted in a split sail when furling. When it did, it meant a job for all hands to shift it and bend a new one.

Then again men of the older school could see no security in the "gingerbread" wire stays and back-stays. The *Merse* (1853) had been fitted in the old style, and when in 1856 my father was transferred to the *Lammermuir*, fitted with all the latest improvements, he was anxious to take his boatswain, a hardy old veteran and an excellent seaman, with him. It meant an increased wage, and the ancient mariner accepted. But when he saw the new ship he shook his head and begged to be allowed to back out. Being asked for a reason, he declared he had no confidence in "them damned fiddlestrings," and had nothing but contempt for reefing-topsails, "same as a girl rolls up a b——y window-blind."

But John Willis's pride in the *Lammermuir* was complete. He would hear of nothing to her disparagement; a fact which was rather amusingly illustrated on one occasion. The paragon's steering-wheel was too small, and old John was informed of it. But he pooh-poohed the idea, the wheel was " a' richt "; nobody knew what they were talking about.

In 1859 he made a trip in the ship and, as his custom was, took full charge. He was delighted when the buoy was slipped at Gravesend, and before a fresh gale at west-south-west his favourite ship reeled off the knots in fine style. He was particularly pleased to pass a new ship belonging to a brother Scot which had been "cracked up" as a possible rival to the unparalleled *Lammermuir*. He rubbed his hands with glee and chuckled hugely: " What wull John Brodie have to say aboot his *Land o' Cakes* noo? "

So far, so good. But on clearing the Prince's Channel the wind freshened and a squall was observed making up to the southward. The pilot suggested taking some canvas off the ship, while the captain ventured to remind his owner of the unreliability of the

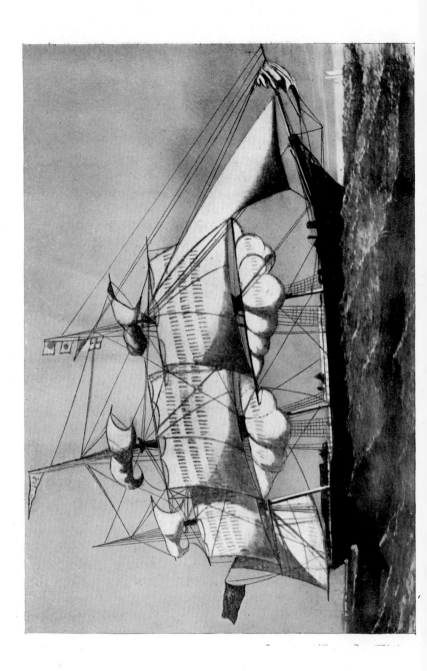

steering-gear. Such remarks were like showing a red rag to a bull. Old John glared at them. " What? " he said. " Are ye afeard? I'll show ye some sea-manship."

Nevertheless, he ordered the lighter sails to be clewed up and stationed hands by the topgallant halyards. Then the squall struck the ship and had more than a capful of wind in it. The *Lammermuir* went over to her bearings, creaking in every fibre aloft and with the main tack surging round the bollards.

Old John cast a glance at the supremely uncon-scious-looking skipper, then gave the order to lower away. It was clear that this would not be enough to make her easy, and old John, forgetting the dispute about the wheel, roared out : " Hard up the helm ! hard up ! "

The helmsman endeavoured to obey the order and others came to his assistance. It was no use; force failed to move it. For a few seconds it looked as though the masts would go. The *Lammermuir* lay down to it and hummed under the pressure. Then, fortunately, the force of the squall spent itself, and the ship came back to something nearer an even keel.

But old John had had enough for one day. He made a sign to the skipper, who was trying not to look cheerful, and disappeared below. There he was heard roaring for the " Steward ! " who was an old servant and could be relied on to produce the proper remedy.

Soon afterwards the ship was brought to anchor in the Downs. Next morning the owner left for home in a Deal hoveller. He bade good-bye to the captain with the usual formula : " Well, good-bye, my boy; tak' care of her, and do the best you can " (in the matter of employment).

Going over the side he hesitated, and in a lower tone added : " And harkee, Shewan, if I should slip

my cable before you come back, tell young John to
gie ye a new wheel."

My father left the *Lammermuir* in 1860, and
thereafter we were less closely in touch with the old
gentleman. By that time, however, age was beginning
to tell, and he left the care of his ships more and more
to his sons, much to the regret of the few old servants
who had followed his fortunes and grown accustomed
to his exacting ways. Yet under his rough exterior he
was very human and likeable. Though plain-living
and careful, he was far from penurious. His ships
were always well found and well manned.

In his latest years, like many another old seafarer,
he took much pleasure in his garden. He loved to sit
and smoke among the fruit and flower trees, as aforetime
in the 'tween-decks of the *Merse* and *Lammermuir*.

It was there his end came. On the 10th of July,
1862, he retired as usual after dinner to his favourite
nook at the end of his long garden for a smoke and
rest. He did not appear at the usual hour and his
daughter Janet went to seek him. She found him
sitting on the garden seat, his handkerchief over
his face. To her call of " Father ! " he made no
response, and when she went nearer to rouse him
she found the spirit had departed. The soul of
John Willis, good old " Stormalong," had taken flight
for a better land.

Almost at the same time his beloved *Lammermuir*
was wrecked in Gaspar Straits. She never wore the
blue ribbon of mourning for the man whose favourite
she was. Thus after a packed and strenuous life, the
end of old John Willis was peace. To him was
granted that petition which comes from many when,
for the last time, the anchor is weighed :

> " Oh, may there be no moaning on the bar,
>   When I put out to sea."

CHAPTER VI

THE first tea race that I remember with any distinctness was that between the *Cairngorm* and *Lammermuir* in 1858.

When the Treaty of Tientsin, which brought the Chinese War to an end, was signed in 1858, and the Canton River was reopened to foreign trade, a number of vessels were waiting in Hong-Kong to load the teas which had been collecting in Whampoa.

Most of the British cracks, *Robin Hood, Friar Tuck, Fiery Cross, Assyrian,* etc., had already left Foochow or Shanghai earlier in the season, but a fine fleet of clippers, both British and American, were awaiting the expected harvest of freights. Among them were the *Cairngorm* and *Lammermuir*, British ships; the *Mandarin, Young America* and *Sweepstakes,* three black-hulled American flyers, and the queenly *Panama* and *Picayune,* also American, both carrying crews composed entirely, with the exception of the captains and officers, of negroes.

The contrast of the black figures of the men with the snow-white cotton canvas which, in common with all Yankee clippers, the latter ships carried, reminded one, when they were furling sail, of the " down-easter's " suggestion for a temporary lighthouse on Cape Cod—" a long nigger with a lump of chalk in his mouth."

59

Among the British ships selected to be " laid on the berth " were Jardine's flyer *Cairngorm*, the *Wynaud*, *Chieftain*, *Morning Star* and *Warrior Queen*. My father's ship, the *Lammermuir*, was also chosen, largely, I think, because her commander had made himself so popular with the Hong-Kong folk in the difficult days they experienced prior to the cessation of hostilities.

All these ships had some reputation for speed, but the pick of the bunch was undoubtedly the famous *Cairngorm*. The *Wynaud*, built for speed and intended as a cruiser for the East India Company's Marine, and the *Chieftain*, a new ship of about six hundred tons built at Garmouth on the Spey, were considered to have a sporting chance. The *Morning Star*, a Dundee-built clipper newly off the stocks, was also expected to give a good account of herself.

A few were ready to back " old Shewan " in the Sunderland-built *Lammermuir*, but the *Warrior Queen* was looked upon as merely an " also ran."

The reputations of the respective masters had something to do with the anticipated results. The commanders of the *Cairngorm*, *Wynaud* and *Lammermuir* were all old stagers. The others were comparative strangers to the trade.

The preponderance of Scottish skippers in the China clippers of the day is a point to be noted. Reid of the *Wynaud*, Shewan of the *Lammermuir* and Jenkins of the *Warrior Queen* all hailed from the little whaling port of Peterhead in Aberdeenshire. Blacklock of the *Chieftain* was a Banffshire man; Forman of the *Morning Star* belonged to Dundee; while Ryrie, to complete the list, hailed from the neighbourhood of Stornoway.

To encourage the masters and mates to " ride to win " a gratuity of about £200 was promised by the shippers, to be divided *pro rata* among the officers of the ship to dock first in London—not, be it noted, for the ship making the fastest passage between port and port.

The *Wynaud* and the *Chieftain*, being of the least tonnage, were, I think, the first to leave. They sailed just ahead of the *Cairngorm*, which left Whampoa on November 6th, followed by the *Lammermuir* on the 8th. The remainder followed close upon their heels, but, as the race early resolved itself into a contest between the *Cairngorm* and the *Lammermuir*, the exact dates are not of much consequence.

The details of the race were for long the subject of animated discussion amongst us.

The ships carried a brisk north-east monsoon past the Paracels and scampered past Pulo Sapata with stunsails spread, alow and aloft. One or two stunsail booms were knocked out of the *Cairngorm* on the passage down the China Sea, and the *Lammermuir* carried away her main topgallant yard scudding before the monsoon.

The *Cairngorm* and the *Wynaud* shaped their course for the Straits of Banca, separating the island of that name from the main of Sumatra; while the *Lammermuir* steered for the Macclesfield, the western-most channel of Gaspar Straits.

The former was considered the safer route, but was somewhat the longer of the two. The coast on both sides of Banca Straits is mostly flat, but should a vessel take the ground there she could be hove off by laying out an anchor, though she ran much risk of being assaulted by Malay pirates in the course of the operation.

The Straits of Gaspar, on the other hand, carry deep water up to the fringing reefs of the many islands, and there are several dangerous sunken rocks in the fairway, notably the Discovery Reefs. The currents, moreover, are strong and variable, and should a ship get ashore the chances were remote she would ever come off again. Such, in fact, was the actual fate of the *Lammermuir* in 1862. She stranded on the Amherst Reef, on the east side of the channel, where she remained visible for many years. I saw her myself in 1874, when her lower masts were still standing; how much longer she lasted I cannot say. The whole neighbourhood had an evil reputation for pirates, and should disaster overtake a vessel, Malay proas would soon be seen gathering for a wrecking expedition.

The *Cairngorm* had a tedious passage through the Straits of Banca, while the *Lammermuir* was more fortunate. She passed through Gaspar Strait into the Java Sea on the tenth day out and, to the surprise of all her company, on the following morning found herself alongside the *Cairngorm*, having gained two clear days on the latter. The *Wynaud* was not far astern.

The ships were now in the region of the north-west monsoon, south of the line, sailing closehauled on the starboard tack, neither making more than two or three knots, the wind being very light.

This was the *Lammermuir's* strong point of sailing, and the Aberdeen clipper's weak one. Like many extremely sharp ships with slightly hollow lines, she became a trifle sluggish in light winds. Thus the rather full-bowed *Lammermuir* gradually gained on her, coming up on the lee quarter. The two captains being good friends, Ryrie hung out a white tablecloth, signifying " Come on board to dinner," and Shewan, nothing loath, lowered his gig and was pulled over to the *Cairngorm*

The mate of the *Lammermuir* at the time was one Francis Moore, a native of Schleswig-Holstein, who had served John Willis almost from boyhood. He had been with my father since 1853, first as second, afterwards as chief mate. He was a first-class seaman and remained in the Willis's employ until about 1878, becoming master of the *Merse* in 1860 and successively commanding the *Whiteadder, Blackadder* and *Cutty Sark*.

Moore was very proud of the *Lammermuir* and saw a chance to execute a manœuvre that would redound to her credit for all time. This was " to go through the lee," as the phrase went, of the crack tea-clipper of the day and sail round her; than which nothing could be more irritating to a proud rival.

Thus while the two captains were below at dinner the *Lammermuir* had so far fore-reached on the *Cairngorm* that Moore was able to put his helm down, come about on the port tack and stand across the bows of the other. Then, on the weather beam of the *Cairngorm,* he tacked once more and resumed his course.

The report of the officer of the watch to Captain Ryrie at the dinner table that the *Lammermuir* was crossing the bows brought the two captains on deck. After the first gasp of surprise, Ryrie was furious. " Well, I'm jiggered! " he gasped, " look at the perishing Dutchman! By the powers! I'll dress him down when I get him ashore."

I do not know whether he had his wish, but at least it was certain he was never able to obliterate the memory of the fact that the *Lammermuir* once sailed round the redoubtable *Cairngorm*.

Through the Straits of Sunda the two ships worked together, well ahead, as it afterwards proved, of any of the others. Once outside Java Head, in the brisk south-east trades of the Indian Ocean, the *Cairngorm* got ahead of the *Lammermuir* and just managed to keep the lead for the rest of the passage.

Anjer town in the Straits of Sunda was passed at night. Malay proas, as usual, were cruising about, laden with fruit and yams, and several of them ran alongside the *Lammermuir*.

The first boatman on board was a Malay well known to tea-clipper seamen as " Paul Jones." Father was busy at the time and asked the mate to purchase from him a supply of eggs.

Mr. Moore did so. A large basketful of eggs was passed aboard in the darkness, a number of dollars changed hands, and the boat pushed off. It was afterwards remembered that Paul did not stay for the purpose of further " trade," but at once " topped his boom " for his native village.

The reason was clear when the cook came to prepare a supply of ham and eggs for next morning's breakfast. The aroma from those eggs nearly raised the roof from the galley. The whole consignment was promptly and irretrievably dumped.

The mate was chaffed unmercifully about his marketing. A controversy was begun as to whether the eggs had been laid " too late " or were the product of very old hens. Moore's contribution to the argument was swear words and a stern resolve to get even with " Paul Jones " next time they foregathered.

To finish the story I may say that eight months later the *Lammermuir* was again passing Anjer, outward bound and with the same officers on board. To the delight of the mate " Paul Jones " once more came alongside, having apparently forgotten his last deal with the ship.

Moore laid his plans; sent along another inquiry for eggs, and, when produced, distributed them to a force in ambush. Then " Paul Jones " was told to lay aft for his money.

He came, to be confronted by the indignant mate, who recapitulated the story of his misdeeds and added a rider on the text: "The way of the transgressor is hard."

A sporting chance was given Paul to reach his boat (but without further payment) through the gauntlet of the port watch, stationed all ready to pelt him with his own " hen fruit."

Paul took it. It was the season of Ramadan, when no good Mahomedan breaks his fast between sunrise and sundown, but I fancy one of "the children of the Prophet" had a taste of " eggs " before he got over the side.

But to get back. The two leaders passed Anjer on November 20th; the *Lammermuir* twelve days from Whampoa, the *Cairngorm* fourteen. The *Wynaud* was not far behind.

Thereafter the *Cairngorm*, as I have said, went ahead and the *Lammermuir* was never in company with her again. She anchored in the Downs just forty hours after her formidable rival, having made the passage in six hours less time. The time taken by each ship was ninety-two days, though I see that Mr. Lubbock, in his " China Clippers," gives that of the *Lammermuir* as ninety-three days. Probably he arrives at this reckoning by recording when the ships entered at the custom-house in London.

The race was considered a great triumph for the *Lammermuir*, to have beaten the crack Aberdeen clipper of the day, if only by six hours. Of course the *Cairngorm* was awarded the bonus promised, but the consignees of the *Lammermuir's* teas were so pleased with her performance, as her cargo came to an equally good market, that they presented the same gratuity to the master and officers as had been given to the *Cairngorm*.

E

The *Wynaud* was third and the *Chieftain* fourth, both ships being under a hundred days. The *Morning Star* was close behind, while the *Warrior Queen* acted as whipper-in, but neither ship was disgraced, as the latter was only twelve days behind the leaders.

MACAO.

Facing p. 66.

CHAPTER VII

ON BOARD THE " WYNAUD "

THE ship to arrive third in the tea race from China in 1858 was the *Wynaud*.

An old friend of mine, Bowling by name, was an apprentice on board at the time and wrote an account of the passage, which may throw some light on the conditions aboard a tea-clipper of the time. His narrative was published in *The Canterbury Times* and it may be that the diction owes something to the editor, for it smacks in places of a more practised hand than that of the Bowling I knew. Still, the facts given are authentic enough. The commander of the *Wynaud*, the Captain Reid he speaks of, I knew intimately, both as a friend of the family and a respected senior in after years.

The *Wynaud* was built for the opium trade, and designed partly as a " pirate catcher," partly as a carrier of the precious drug. She was armed with six nine-pounder guns—a larger armament than that of most tea-clippers of the fifties. The majority carried only two iron guns of small calibre, though they had plenty of muskets, pistols, cutlasses and boarding pikes. " She also carried a gunner; and gun drill was regularly carried out by the crew, small as it was, so that, when coming down the China seas, they were all in readiness and well-equipped for a tussle with the night-prowling proas of the Malay seas, or the junks of the sneaky and cut-throat Chinamen.

67

" Many a ship mysteriously disappeared from the face of the waters in those days, but though nothing was ever heard of them, there was little doubt in the minds of sailors as to their fate, supposing they had not got clear of the Malay islands.

" All vessels that could do so reported at Anjer Point; and there a sort of record was kept of all ships entering and leaving the Malay and China waters. ' Pirates got her ' was the verdict on a missing ship.

" Sometimes the Chinese or Malay pirate craft, coming along under their long sweeps, would surprise a vessel in a calm at the dead of night; sometimes a ship would run aground in these shallow waters, and then from the creeks and coves of the nearby land flocks of swift proas, crowded with murderous gangs, would dash down upon her. The fights put up by the white crews would be brave and desperate; but the numbers of their ferocious opponents would prevail. The end was always the same, once the pirates took the ship. ' Dead men tell no tales,' and every soul, passengers as well as sailors, would be murdered, the ship looted of all valuables, and then burned, scuttled and sunk."

Bowling asserts that pirates were an ever present and real danger during the time of his service in the Wynaud, especially in narrow waters. " After working down," he says, " through the China Sea, with the forest-hung mountains of Borneo on the port hand, the clipper would pass through Banca or Gaspar Straits, into the Java Sea.

" All these waters, reef-dotted and shoal-infested, and the coasts of the great islands that hemmed in the narrow seas, wooded from the water's edge to their cloudy summits, swarmed with pirates of the Malay and China breeds. Borneo, Sumatra, Java, Banca,

Billiton, Lombok and a hundred smaller islands harboured their ruffians of the seas; and when the wind came ahead in restricted waters, and the ship had to anchor to save herself from being swept back or shorewards by the strong currents, a close and anxious watch was kept for the silently-stealing proas.

" Sometimes it was necessary to anchor in deep water, in sixty or eighty fathoms [*sic*]. Sometimes again the anchor was let go for the night so close to the islands of Banca or Sumatra that monkeys could be heard chattering in the trees, and the tropic birds singing or screaming; while the roar of the tiger might be heard, as ' Stripes ' came down to drink at some creek mouth."

On such occasions an armed anchor watch was kept —one man with a loaded rifle on the poop, and another, similarly armed, on the forecastle head, with orders to fire the instant any boat was seen approaching. The guns were kept ready loaded, and a poker always heated in the galley. The *Wynaud's* crew at that time fired their guns in the primitive manner— with powder on the touch hole and a red-hot iron. Later on, Bowling says, cartridges were served out, fired by detonators. He does not mention that a supply of boiling water was always kept on the galley fire, ready to repel boarders; yet this was a practice conformed to in nearly all the clippers. The shot used was canister and grape, the most effective projectiles for crowded proas.

Bowling goes on to give a description of a young sailor's duties on board the *Wynaud*, which may be taken as true of the tea-clippers generally.

" The intricate navigation, with the arduous seamanship required in those perilous waters, and the necessity for warlike precautions, gave the master mariners of the China clippers of those days an anxious time until they had cleared the Straits of Sunda and left the pirate nests astern.

" In the China Sea the weather was often shockingly bad—rain in tropical sheets, thunder and lightning terrible in their intensity. We would be wet through all day, and whenever the wind came fair it was out with the stunsails. No possible chance was lost, for it was always a race.

" We boys used to be roused out in our watch below to set topgallant and royal stunsails; and we would be perched aloft, reeving and unreeving gear, and setting and taking in the sails, half a dozen times a day."

The royal and topgallant stunsails, I should say, were stowed in the " round tops " triced up against the topmast rigging, and it was the boys' prerogative, which they would gladly have foregone, to drag the sails into the tops when taken in, and to shake them out ready for setting again. It was an operation not easily to be carried out by a greenhorn, as Bowling observes.

" A delicate bit of work," he describes it, " and an accomplishment that is now altogether lost." Quite true. I had about five years of it and I do not know any job better calculated to teach a boy to swear than this same performance of getting a heavy topgallant stunsail into a top, particularly when the yards had been hauled round after the sail had been taken in, and the whole iniquitous contraption was jammed by the lee gear. With a wet sail into the bargain, and an inconsiderate mate yelling out for one's presence on deck, he was more a saint than a sailor who could forbear to curse.

" We youngsters," says Bowling, and I can re-echo him, " had plenty of practice in the art in those days. There was no watch below in the afternoon for us boys at any time. The lead was always kept going when

working through risky passages. Old Captain Reid
would not trust the men to heave the lead, but kept his
apprentices at it; there was always one of the boys in
the mizzen chains, swinging the deep-sea lead."

" Deep-sea " lead, Bowling says, but this is surely
an oversight—no boy would be asked to swing the deep-
sea lead. In cases like this it was the seven-pound hand
lead which was used. When the thirty-pound deep-sea,
or dipsey, lead was used and the ship was moving ahead,
the whole watch was required, as the lead had to be
passed well forward before being dropped into the water.
The leadsman who took the soundings was stationed
well aft, while two or more hands were posted on the
rail between the heaver and the leadsman. They kept
the line in their hands until the strain came upon it,
when they let go, each man in turn calling out:
" Watch, there, watch." The idea was that the lead
should be on the ground when the motion of the ship
brought it opposite the leadsman.

To effect this, the distance the lead was carried
forward was proportionate to the depth of water expected
and the speed of the ship. In water over twenty
fathoms deep it would be necessary to stop the way of
the ship entirely to obtain a correct sounding.

A single man in the chains swinging the hand lead
was only used when in shoal water, say under ten
fathoms, when it was feared that the ship might run
into a dangerous shallow at any moment. Bowling
speaks of being kept at the task for " many hours," but
usually " the man in the chains," like " the man at the
wheel," was relieved every two hours.

" Old Captain Reid," he continues, " would be
lying down in his long chair on the poop. ' Now then,
youngster,' he would say, ' what watter hae ye gotten ? '
When there was a longer interval than usual between
the apprentice's reports: ' Dom it ! ' he would shout,

' are ye asleep? ' The old man thought a lot of his boys, though he made them work like niggers. ' Ah! ' he would say, ' ye'll nae gang awa' frae me and say I didna mak' sailors o' ye.' "

Such was the navigation of the long, tortuous Banca Straits. No leadsman was needed in the chains in the Macclesfield, as deep water is there carried right up to the edge of the reefs, which could generally be seen in time to put the ship about. The various scattered sunken reefs had to be given a wide berth, but their position was accurately determined by cross bearings of well defined points of land. No prudent master would attempt the Macclesfield at night; there were no leading lights in the Straits then, and a ship would be brought to anchor while in safety to wait for daylight.

With due deference to Captain Bowling's remarks about pirates, I think that what he says, at least about the Malay variety, was somewhat traditional, even in 1858. Captain Whidden, an American shipmaster, writing some dozen years previously, says that matters had improved considerably in that direction, even in his day. Fights with Borneo Dyaks, moving about in large fleets, were growing infrequent. Yet it was true enough the *terror* of them had by no means disappeared, and shipmasters took every precaution, especially when navigating Banca Straits, as I know from personal experience even as late as 1865.

Stranding was the misadventure most dreaded. Crews were loath to stand by their helpless ships in that neighbourhood of evil reputation, when scattered Malay proas might be seen dodging off each point and cape, ready to muster for an attack.

Yet I remember one occasion when a ship's company were a bit previous in abandoning their stranded vessel. It happened about the year 1868; twenty years earlier

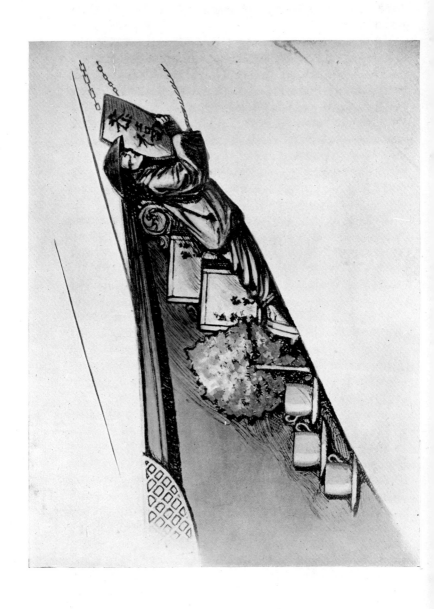

there would have been much better justification for their action.

In that year two clippers, the *Fusiyama* and *Maggie Leslie,* left Shanghai together for London with tea.

The leading ship, the *Maggie Leslie* I think it was, but I write from memory and am not quite certain, when about a day's sail ahead of the other, ran ashore on Pulo Leat in Gaspar Straits. As night was approaching and another vessel was in company, the officers and crew, thinking under the circumstances " safety first " was as good a motto as another, transferred themselves to the passing stranger and abandoned the unlucky tea-clipper to her fate.

However, her time was not yet come. By some means, possibly a rising tide coinciding with a squall off the island, she floated off the reef and, having her canvas still set, drifted clear.

Next morning her rival came along and, to the surprise of all on board, found their competitor " backing and filling " in mid-channel with not a soul on board.

Here was a fine opportunity for prize money, and those on board the *Fusiyama* seized it. An officer with a few hands was sent on board the derelict, and the two ships proceeded in company to Batavia.

The choice of this port was a mistake on the part of the salvors. Had the abandoned vessel been kept at sea, while the rescuing ship picked up a few hands at Batavia or Anjer—natives would have done, if European seamen were not available—and then navigated to London, her port of destination, the salvage money would have been vastly greater than what was awarded at Batavia. Even as it was, a substantial salvage ensued, the share of each A.B. being over £20.

Regarding the chattering of monkeys and roaring of tigers on the Banca coasts at night that Bowling speaks of, I do not think he is exaggerating. Many seamen stated they had heard them, but not to the extent of an old salt who used to spin me long yarns of the Indian seas in my boyhood days at Blackwall. He was particularly loquacious on the subject of the Straits of Bally-bang-jang (Balambangan), where, he said, they were unable to swing the yards on account of monkeys' tails getting jammed in the brace blocks.

But, as I say, that was before my time.

CHAPTER VIII

BUILDING THE " CHAA-SZE "

IN 1860 my father was commissioned by Messrs. Turner & Company, tea merchants in Canton, to buy or build a clipper-ship for the purpose of transporting their early teas to London. The southern port was then Messrs. Turner's headquarters, though, conservative as they were, they were compelled a year or two later to abandon it in favour of Foochow.

As time was precious father fixed on a smart little clipper then on the stocks at Alexander Hall & Sons' yard at Aberdeen. She had been ordered by a Peterhead firm and intended for a steam whaler, but a couple of unsuccessful seasons had landed the concern in bankruptcy and Hall's were left " holding the baby."

However, it was not for long. When my father, a willing buyer, arrived he found a willing seller, and mutually satisfactory terms were speedily arranged.

It was customary in those days to send an experienced seaman to overlook the construction of a new ship. His advice might be useful on a number of points, and he could be trusted, moreover, to be satisfied with nothing short of the best workmanship in the vessel he was to command.

There were many details which required the closest scrutiny. Wormholes in teak planking and treenail holes which had been overlooked were fruitful sources of after trouble. The latter might be productive of disaster. The hole which had been bored for a treenail might become filled up with sawdust and so be overlooked—to result afterwards in a leak.

It may not be superfluous, in these days of steel ships, to explain that treenails, or trunnels, were cylindrical pins of hardwood such as greenheart, used to secure the planking to the frames, or the parts to each other. They required considerable effort to drive home, though not nearly so much as that necessary to force a copper or yellow-metal bolt, some four or five feet in length, through keelson and keel or breasthooks and stem. The insertion of such a thing took several days and was attacked at intervals before it was finally driven home.

By the fifties suitable timber for the frames and beams of large ships was growing scarce. This had led to the introduction of " diagonal building," in which heavier planking was used, to permit the frames to be spaced much farther apart. A " diagonal-built " ship usually had two thicknesses of planking running diagonally from the keel to the plank sheer, crossing each other at right-angles, while a third thickness (the outside one) was carried fore and aft.

Thus there were nine inches of planking to be fastened together in the spaces between the frames. It came to be considered that the smooth, cylindrical treenail did not take a sufficient grip of the three separate planks, and this led to the introduction of " screw " treenails. These were of the same material, but " wormed," with a square head which permitted them to be screwed in with a spanner. They were a novelty in 1860, and much interest was taken in those inserted in the *Chaa-sze*. When I was in Aberdeen in 1924 I was shown one which the firm keep as a memento.

In the *Chaa-sze* the teak frames were from four to

six feet apart, with a triple thickness of planking, binding the whole together into nine inches of solid teak. Indeed, the ship was so tightly bound that later several of her lower deck beams were made to unship to give her more play.

This idea, as the late Mr. Edwards has recorded, " came from a trick of the old slavers which, when hard pressed by a cruiser, would saw through their deck beams in order to improve their sailing. On one occasion the *Chaa-sze* was in company, off Mauritius, with the Sunderland clipper, *Chanticleer*, both bound for China. They had been together for four days, in light, variable winds. Suddenly a steady breeze arrived and the *Chaa-sze* at once forged ahead. ' There she goes,' cried the ' Geordie ' skipper of the *Chanticleer*, ' they have unscrewed the beams and we shan't see her again.' No more they did."

As far as her model was concerned the new ship had all the requirements of a tea-clipper. Her lines had been taken off the model of the famous *Robin Hood*, though her tonnage was considerably less. She was a very graceful craft and gave no indication from her appearance that she had ever been intended for a " blubber hunter." As for her queer name, her owners were themselves " tea-tasters " and chose the Chinese equivalent for that profession as the title of their new clipper.

In keeping therewith her figurehead consisted of two reclining Celestials, supporting a shield on which was depicted the name in Chinese characters; while trailing along the cutwater were representations of tea-chests, teapots, cups and saucers, including a weird-looking object like " a birch broom in a fit," which was intended to represent a tea shrub.

I fancy my father was responsible for this work of art, though he had to depend on Aberdeen artists for its portrayal in wood, and " honour to whom honour is due." It was much admired and the figures were considered to be excellent portraits of " Ah-Sin."

But it was my intention to describe the launching of the *Chaa-sze,* and I have already been guilty of a serious mistake. It was considered most unlucky to give away the name of a new ship before she was ceremonially christened. I remember that at the time father himself unwittingly almost " sold the pass " in this manner.

Whilst the *Chaa-sze* was still on the stocks several vessels were launched from neighbouring yards. Amongst them was a fine little ship, the *Marquis of Argyle,* so named after the nobleman who fell a victim to his covenanting principles in the days of the royal Stewarts. She was built for a dour Presbyterian, who owned a fleet of vessels all named after prominent leaders of reform,—*John Knox, Martin Luther, John Bunyan,* etc.

At the launch of the *Marquis* this gentleman encountered my father and casually inquired : " And what are ye to ca' your new ship, Shewan ? " The forbidden word was on the tip of father's tongue, but he recollected himself in time and substituted another, also beginning with a " C."

" We thocht o' ca'in' her the *Claverhoose,*" he said gravely.

The name of the " Bluidy Claver'se," the relentless persecutor of the Covenanters, was about to provoke a wrathful rejoinder, when the other remembered the superstition and laughed. " Awa' wi' ye and your havers, Shewan," said he, " I ken you weel."

My first trip in a tea-clipper was not of long duration. It was simply a glide, gradually increasing in speed, down the launching ways of Hall's yard, as the ship made her graceful curtsy to the silvery Dee and followed it up with a grand rush to the opposite river-bank. Then she was brought up by her straining cables and the great anchors half-buried in the ground ashore.

There was not much room for launches at the Aberdeen yards and great care had to be taken that the anchors would do the work required. It would, of course, have been easy enough to have buried them so that they were immovable. But chain cables do not stretch much, and snap easily. The strain, therefore, was eased by allowing the anchors to plough their way through the gravel and so bring the vessel to a standstill gently. At the same time it was vital for the ship's way to be stopped before her sternpost touched the boulders fronting the " Inches," or untoward damage would ensue. Some capable men, therefore, were stationed by the anchors with baulks of timber to bring the launch to a standstill at the critical moment. This was considered so important that I noticed William Hall himself taking the lead in the operations here.

The *Chaa-sze* was launched with her rudder shipped, and the cables led through the hawse-pipes ready for service; but at a launch I witnessed on the Wear a few weeks later the means used to bring the vessel up afforded much more excitement to the spectators.

This was at the launch of the great 1,400-ton frigate-built ship *Malabar*, built for Green's of Blackwall. There seemed to be even less room for launching at Sunderland than was the case at Aberdeen and every precaution was taken.

The *Malabar* had no rudder shipped, but abaft her sternpost a great perpendicular baulk of timber, making a false sternpost, was secured, and the cables that were to check the ship's way were not led through the hawse-pipes, but along the vessel's sides and round this sternpost.

We were accommodated at a window almost in line

of her career, which, however, many were inclined to attribute to the unwisdom of splicing a " heathen " name on to a " Christian " ceremony.

As was customary, one or two of the more youthful carpenters had concealed themselves on board the ship in the bows, to make prize of the silk ribbons and rosettes left hanging there; these tokens being much valued by the bonnie lasses of Aberdeen. I remember seeing the lucky man on this occasion defending his spoils from marauding comrades, each eager for a yard or two of the ribbon as a means of winning a smile from some bashful maiden.

After the launch, a second ceremony of a different nature was successfully carried out, which may have helped to avert some of the evil caused by the first failure. This certainly seems to be a survival from heathen rites. If in the first case we may assume that wine was substituted for blood, in the second it may be that the immersion and whipping of youths took the place of death by drowning in ancient times, or of being crushed under the vessel as she slid down the ways— a sacrifice to some vindictive " shark-god."

This custom, as it was carried out at the launch of the *Chaa-sze*, and as I have further witnessed it at the launching of Peterhead whalers, consisted in the ducking, and sometimes thrashing, of ship carpenters' apprentices; or, indeed, of any unlucky greenhorns who could be inveigled to the water's edge.

As the ship left the ways two or more stalwart shipwrights took up positions by the waterside, and, at the critical moment, seized any victims within reach and plunged them head over heels into the recoiling wave thrown up by the vessel's passage into the water. They were ducked not once but three times, unless they were agile enough to escape; and I have been told by an old Aberdonian that he has seen unfortunate youths river-bank. Then she was brought up by her straining cables and the great anchors half-buried in the ground ashore.

There was not much room for launches at the Aberdeen yards and great care had to be taken that the anchors would do the work required. It would, of course, have been easy enough to have buried them so that they were immovable. But chain cables do not stretch much, and snap easily. The strain, therefore, was eased by allowing the anchors to plough their way through the gravel and so bring the vessel to a standstill gently. At the same time it was vital for the ship's way to be stopped before her sternpost touched the boulders fronting the " Inches," or untoward damage would ensue. Some capable men, therefore, were stationed by the anchors with baulks of timber to bring the launch to a standstill at the critical moment. This was considered so important that I noticed William Hall himself taking the lead in the operations here.

The *Chaa-sze* was launched with her rudder shipped, and the cables led through the hawse-pipes ready for service; but at a launch I witnessed on the Wear a few weeks later the means used to bring the vessel up afforded much more excitement to the spectators.

This was at the launch of the great 1,400-ton frigate-built ship *Malabar*, built for Green's of Blackwall. There seemed to be even less room for launching at Sunderland than was the case at Aberdeen and every precaution was taken.

The *Malabar* had no rudder shipped, but abaft her sternpost a great perpendicular baulk of timber, making a false sternpost, was secured, and the cables that were to check the ship's way were not led through the hawse-pipes, but along the vessel's sides and round this sternpost.

We were accommodated at a window almost in line

with the vessel's course. She came across grandly, presenting a noble appearance. Large crowds had assembled and were cheering wildly at the sight. The cheers ceased suddenly as flashes of fire were seen to come from the tautening cables at the stern, and, with a terrific crashing and rending, the great baulks of timber protecting the stern frame were shivered into matchwood, and the lordly vessel was brought to a standstill with her quarter galleries almost overhanging the edge of the quay.

Later in the same year I saw a yet more important launch. This was the *Warrior*, the first of the iron-clads, which took the water from Mear's yard on Bow Creek in the Thames. Here also there was little space, and the vessel was launched diagonally at a bend of the creek.

It was an imposing spectacle; albeit one that for a few seconds looked as though it were going to prove fatal to a number of sightseers, myself included. We had walked across the marshes to the river-wall, a low, earthen embankment bordering the creek, and were cheering vociferously as the great fabric, some 6,000 tons, took the water.

Then a cry of alarm rose from our foremost ranks as a great wave of water, raised by the ship, swept towards us. Fortunately the wave only overtopped the bank in a few hollow places, and we suffered no more than a wild stampede, but, had it breached the wall, we were rushing out of the frying-pan into the fire, for there was a broad ditch before us which would infallibly have swallowed us up. A somewhat similar accident, unfortunately with fatal consequences, did occur at the launch of the *Thunderer* from the same yard.

Our enjoyment at the launch of the *Chaa-sze* was slightly damped by the fear that she might turn turtle. Against father's wishes, we had been given permission to stay on board the ship, and had ensconced ourselves well forward in proximity to the bottle of wine, decorated with rosettes, dangling from the knightheads. Under the figurehead was a railed-in platform, intended for the lady and the party with her who were to perform the ceremony.

Then a clattering of mauls proclaimed that the retaining supports were being knocked away. They continued until only the " dog shores " holding the cradle in which the ship rested were left in position. Then they ceased, and the order was given to " Stand clear ! ".

All being ready, these last preventers were speedily knocked away and the vessel slowly began to move. The lady who was to christen her, repeating a certain formula (which I have forgotten), revealed to the many listeners the hitherto-concealed name. At the same time she swung the bottle towards the ship with intent to break it and spill the wine over the bow.

But alas ! unnerved perhaps by the shouting of the carpenters, or hypnotized by the solemn visages of the Celestials overhead, the lady lost her head and pulled the cord with insufficient force. The bottle swung back without touching the ship, still intact, its mission unfulfilled.

This was a disastrous thing to happen. It was an omen of the very worst kind; and had it not been for the action of a gigantic carpenter, who, springing on a log, managed to seize the wine flask and to swing it with such force that it was dashed into smithereens against the ship's side, the *Chaa-sze* would have taken the water practically a doomed ship.

Even as it was, it could only be called a bungled ceremony; and perhaps to this mishap may be attributed the fact that the *Chaa-sze* was never a " lucky ". ship. She met with a number of misfortunes in the course

F

of her career, which, however, many were inclined to attribute to the unwisdom of splicing a " heathen " name on to a " Christian " ceremony.

As was customary, one or two of the more youthful carpenters had concealed themselves on board the ship in the bows, to make prize of the silk ribbons and rosettes left hanging there; these tokens being much valued by the bonnie lasses of Aberdeen. I remember seeing the lucky man on this occasion defending his spoils from marauding comrades, each eager for a yard or two of the ribbon as a means of winning a smile from some bashful maiden.

After the launch, a second ceremony of a different nature was successfully carried out, which may have helped to avert some of the evil caused by the first failure. This certainly seems to be a survival from heathen rites. If in the first case we may assume that wine was substituted for blood, in the second it may be that the immersion and whipping of youths took the place of death by drowning in ancient times, or of being crushed under the vessel as she slid down the ways— a sacrifice to some vindictive " shark-god."

This custom, as it was carried out at the launch of the *Chaa-sze*, and as I have further witnessed it at the launching of Peterhead whalers, consisted in the ducking, and sometimes thrashing, of ship carpenters' apprentices; or, indeed, of any unlucky greenhorns who could be inveigled to the water's edge.

As the ship left the ways two or more stalwart shipwrights took up positions by the waterside, and, at the critical moment, seized any victims within reach and plunged them head over heels into the recoiling wave thrown up by the vessel's passage into the water. They were ducked not once but three times, unless they were agile enough to escape; and I have been told by an old Aberdonian that he has seen unfortunate youths chased dripping wet half-way up the street, and, when caught, brought back and ducked until it was deemed their baptism had been sufficiently thorough.

At the launch of the *Chaa-sze* the waterside ceremony was carried out with more vim than usual, as a generous allowance of the wine of the country, otherwise " fuskie," had been made to the carpenters engaged thereon.

For the select guests a banquet was provided, at which champagne figured; while another function, dignified with the name of " ball," was held in the evening, to which the wives and sweethearts of all the workmen were invited.

Altogether a launching-day in the " fittie " (Footdee) district of Aberdeen was quite in the nature of a gala. Bunting was everywhere generously displayed, as well on the vessel herself when she emerged from under her shed, as on flagstaffs erected all round the yard.

The first flag to be flung to the breeze, after the British Ensign, was the burgee—a long triangular flag on which the ship's name appeared in bold letters, to apprise all and sundry the hitherto undivulged secret. Yet when the *Chaa-sze's* burgee was seen and read the spectators were not much the wiser—no one could make either head or tail of it. A guess was hazarded that the ship was designed to " chaw " the " sea," and that there was uncertainty how to spell it.

It was generally understood that a bottle of champagne was always broken over the bows of each vessel launched. William Hall's office-boy gave away the secret and revealed the fact that on such occasions his master sent him to a certain grocer's with " one shillun " to purchase a bottle of " christening wine."

Ships' carpenters in those days were willing to do work which would appear much *infra dig* to the trade unionist of to-day. For example, as the *Chaa-sze* proved a wee bit " crank " and quick dispatch was a prime object, that same afternoon the shipwrights hove on board all the ship's cables and stowed them away in the chain lockers, in order that the lower masts might be stepped the following day. They also wheeled the masts from the yard to the sheerlegs on the quay in readiness, afterwards manning capstan and winches to heave them on board. I should say that iron masts had not yet been adopted in sailing-ships, and those of the *Chaa-sze* were of immense weight. They were of teak and " built," it being difficult to find single spars the necessary size and strength.

The *Chaa-sze* was also equipped with a new form of windlass, which had only been fitted to one vessel previously. It operated by means of a capstan on the forecastle head, and made for much easier work than the exhausting " up and down " movement of the wind-lasses then in general use. Much labour was saved, too, when coming to an anchor. There was no need to range chain before the windlass. The barrel over which the cable passed could be unlocked from the main part of the windlass and controlled by a powerful brake operated by a single man.

With the windlass hitherto in use it was necessary, or at all events prudent, to range forty or fifty fathoms of cable on deck, and then have enough of this fleeted round the barrel and ranged before the windlass. It had to be of sufficient scope to allow the anchor to find bottom when let go and so obviate a sudden jerk on the windlass, which would put the instrument out of action at once.

The old type of windlass was merely a cylindrical log, which was made to revolve by handspikes inserted in holes at the ends. The cables were passed round the middle section in one or more turns. When heaving in and some two or three fathoms had been gained, the

A "GEORDIE" BRIG.

Photo. by W. H. Elliott.

cable encroached on the centre of the barrel and it became necessary to " fleet " it. To effect this, the cable had to be stoppered with the " devil's claws " before the windlass, and the turns on the barrel shifted along by hand—a time-wasting, back-breaking operation.

Then again, when a heavier strain than usual came on the cable, it was apt to render round the barrel, so a luff tackle had to be rigged abaft the windlass to keep the chain taut.

At such times the crew were divided into two gangs, while the boys were employed in hauling the chain back and ranging it on the deck as it was hove in. The holes in each end of the windlass into which the bars were shipped were so arranged that when one side was heaving the other was shifting bars. It required much experience to get a good purchase on the handspike when shipped. As it had to be grasped high up one had to spring for it, and old sailors made merry over the ludicrous mishaps of the uninitiated. Failure to spring at the right moment resulted either in missing the handspike and coming a cropper on deck, or receiving a crack on the head from the descending bar which sent one there.

There was little wonder that shipmasters sometimes grew impatient during the process of heaving in and cried : " Slip the confounded thing ! " trusting to recover the anchor later by means of buoy and buoy-rope.

On the *Chaa-sze* Emerson and Walker's patent was dubbed an instant success, and the crew were lost in admiration at " Chips " doing all the work himself, leaving them free to " clew up and furl."

As a matter of fact, it proved its efficiency more triumphantly a couple of years later, when, in 1862, it enabled the *Chaa-sze* to ride safely through the most

severe typhoon ever recorded on the Canton River.
On that occasion she was the only ship in Whampoa
Reach which did not drag her anchors, and this by
reason of the advantages conferred on her by the new
type of windlass. Her two cables were paid out to the
bitter end and were eased off steadily by means of the
lever-brakes, without the jerks calculated to start the
anchor or snap the cable, which could hardly be
avoided in the older forms.

During this typhoon many vessels were driven
ashore, and some were left high and dry among the
paddy fields when the tidal wave subsided. It was
estimated that 60,000 Chinese lost their lives. For long
the river was cumbered with dead bodies. They floated
up with the flood and down with the ebb, and stranded
at low water on the flats.

" Drowned persons," say the Chinese, " belong
joss pidgin " ; that is to say, were the peculiar property
of God and must not be interfered with. But European
opinion thought otherwise, and became so alarmed at
the consequences which must inevitably ensue that they
prevailed on the Chinese authorities to act and offer
a reward for each dead body brought ashore for burial.

The result beggars description. Hundreds of craft
were engaged plying about, towing strings of corpses
behind them. All who have lain on board ship in the
rivers of China or the Hooghli will recall the gruesome
memory when just one dead body floated past. So I
will leave it to their imagination what it was like when
corpses were floating about in hundreds. No one who
was in Canton that year will ever forget it.

I have heard John Willis Junior, he of the famous white hat, tell a story about the *St. Abbs*, which he commanded for two voyages to China. In 1848 when she was built (before the repeal of the Navigation Laws), the *St. Abbs* had been considered a smart little vessel, though, compared with later clippers, I hardly know whether to call her tea-" clipper " or tea-" wagon."

One voyage, Willis said, while loading tea at Whampoa, he had been made aware of a peculiarity in her construction. Ah-Poo, the Chinese stevedore, came up out of the hold one day, with consternation on his face, and sought the captain :

" Me no savee what fashion this ship belong," he said.

" Why, what's wrong with her? "

" This piecee ship velly culious : port side foll-mast me stow thirteen piecee box tea; stal-bord side no can puttie mo' 'an twal piecee."

" Rubbish," said Captain Willis, but he went down to investigate. Sure enough, the stevedore was right. In the fore 'tween decks one more package of tea could be stowed on the port side of the foremast than on the starboard. There was no doubt, as young John proclaimed, that the ship his father was so fond of was lopsided, though whether she was built that way or had been squeezed out of shape I cannot say.

The *Merse* had been laid down for Willis Junior, but he was at sea when she was finished, and on his return home his health was poor and he stayed ashore to carry on with the city side of the business.

Thus it came about that my father took over the command of the *Merse* as soon as she was launched. She was, I think, the first of Willis's ships that could be classed as a clipper, and came in for much admiration when she was new. But vast improvements were made in the tea-clipper model in the course of the next dozen years. In the year 1869 I remember seeing the old vessel alongside the *Norman Court* and the *Cutty Sark*. With her heavy hemp rigging and old-fashioned lines it was hard to realize she was the admired beauty of only fifteen years before. Ships changed much between '50 and '70.

Among the others, the *Janet Willis* had only a short life. She was lost with all hands, and her actual fate was never known.

But to return to Sunderland. What differentiated the north-east coast port from other shipbuilding centres was the presence of its fleet of collier brigs. They were the striking feature of the place, and a fine training ground for local seamen, though a pretty hard one.

Particularly was this the case with the " boys." Besides their ordinary duties the boys had additional service to render to the men forward. They had to bring them their food from the galley, wash up plates and pannikins after meals, and perform other duties obnoxious to high-spirited youth. It used to be said that if a man wanted a drink of water and were sitting on the water cask he would holloa for the " boy " to come and draw it for him. Life was a serious business to a boy brought up in a north-country brig.

There was a warning story told about this. In one " Geordie " brig the unfortunate boy, who also acted as cook, had a particularly rough time of it at the hands of the A.B.'s. The ship reached London and in the evening, after the men had gone ashore, the boy, taking, as it was supposed, the ship's cat with him, deserted. On their return to the ship the crew cursed the boy for stealing their pet, but consoled themselves by attacking the stew for supper that the young rascal had had the grace to leave on the galley fire.

The soup was rich and its unwonted " hairiness "
was attributed to the careless habits of the wretched
boy. But alas! at the bottom of the kettle a mass of
skin and bones was revealed, which threw a sudden
and lurid light on the fate of the cat and the reason
of the boy's departure. " Revenge is sweet " and
that boy must have drunk deep of it. The unfortunate
crew were known ever after as " the men who scoffed
the kitten."

There were many good-natured laughs at the
expense of " Geordie " seamen and their rough and
ready methods.

Some of the Tyne brigs made an occasional voyage
to Quebec for timber, and the master of one borrowed
a quadrant for the trip.

On the way across he determined to " take an
oblikew " and sent the boy below for the instrument.
Having successfully " shot " the sun he proceeded
below and drew many weird geometrical figures on
the chart. The chart itself was something of a novelty
on such craft, whose masters, for the most part, trusted
to the deep sea lead and their native sea-sense.

At last he made an emphatic dig at the chart and
with an air of satisfaction turned to the attendant boy :
" Eh, George, what d'ye think o' that? What would
your mither gie to ken whaur we are noo? "

But George was a dullard and unimpressed. He
scratched his head : " Eh, skipper," he said, " and
what would we gie if we kenned whaur we are
oorsells ? "

But there was another side to " Geordie " sea-life,
and it should be recorded that in danger or disaster,
when the vessel was bumping on a sandbank or hammer-
ing her life out on a rocky coast, it was always the
" boy," and likely enough the cat, who were first passed
into the lifeboat or sent ashore in the breeches-buoy.

CHAPTER X

OWING to the fact that in 1860 the seamen of
Aberdeen were organizing themselves into a protective
society, the *Chaa-sze* had difficulty in obtaining a crew
on her first passage to London. The difficulty was at
length overcome by obtaining a dozen or so of the
younger members of a whaler's crew which had just
returned to Peterhead " a clean ship," that is, with
little or no " blubber." These men signed on instead
of a more orthodox deep water crew; though not
without frequent collisions with the local members of
the union, who were indignant at having the tables
turned upon them. Several free fights took place, in
which the " ship " forces were generally victorious,
and the whalemen sailed in the ship. It was represented
that the *Chaa-sze* being a clipper, would return in time
for them to sail in the 1861 Greenland fleet—a promise
that, though they thought it scarcely possible at the
time, actually came to pass.

The " Greenlanders " were a fine crowd, though
in character very different to the usual run of clipper
seamen. Father was well aware of the wild nature of
his countrymen and warned the mate not to expect too
much from them at first in the way of discipline. The
mate was Archie Donald, a keen disciplinarian, who
had been trained in the Aberdeen White Star Line
and was afterwards master of the clipper *Queen of*

Nations. He was lost overboard a few years later while running down the easting on the way to Australia.

The " whalemen " were little versed in the niceties of sea-discipline, and apt to consider " Jack was as good as his master." Their first lesson in sea-etiquette, coming from the burly second mate, took them by surprise. Mr. Watt was himself a native of Peterhead and had sailed several voyages in the whalers. Though hardly to be called a " Beau Brummell," he was on his dignity as an " offisher " in a tea-clipper. To his orders or inquiries the men responded briefly with " Aye " or " Nae "—the addition " Sir " being quite unknown on the north-east coast. Besides, they had known Mr. Watt from youth.

Mr. Watt took each unconscious delinquent to task. " Look here, ye maun jist mind that aboord this ship I hae a handle to my name. I'm Mr. Watt tae ye, and when I tell ye to dae anything, ye maun say, ' Aye, aye, sir '—d'ye ken?—Aye, aye, *sir*." Each of his auditors in turn gaped at him, but slowly assimilated the information. It was a vast surprise to them; at home they had been wont to call the gentleman " Truff Watt," or more simply " Truff."

The peculiar conditions of their life had made them splendid " hard weather " seamen, but in fine weather they were by no means easy to manage. Accustomed as they were to a short cruise, and comparatively a merry one, varying their shipboard duties with chasing whales and clubbing seals, generously supplied with food and grog, knowing, too, that the harder they worked the bigger would be the pay-day they would have to handle, they grew restive at the monotony of tropical weather in a long-voyage merchantman.

The rationing of food was a thing they could never be brought to understand, and there would have been trouble had they been asked to put up with the skinflint fare of some ships. Fortunately in the *Chaa-sze* they had nothing to complain of on this score. The ship was well supplied with provisions, and their commander was a man of an entirely different disposition to a certain notorious shipmaster who denied his men potatoes and defended his action on the ground that " tatties were ower guid a pilot tae the beef."

I do not mean to say that there was any insubordination on their part, simply a freedom and truculence of demeanour that was not often encountered on board the clippers. It was natural enough among the " sea boys " of a Greenlandman. There, among the ice-floes, the hazards of harpooning and lancing a whale, made rank as such of little account. A lubberly action on the part of an officer would be as disappointing or disastrous as on the part of a man. Instead of wages, each man received a " share," and the skill or incompetence of each member of the ship's company was directly reflected in the pocket of each of his comrades. The fact made for plain-speaking and an entire absence of mere politeness.

On the other hand, in moments of peril or emergency, no more welcome shipmates could be imagined than the Greenlandmen. An instance in proof of this occurred on this same first voyage of the *Chaa-sze*.

The ship at the time was working to the northward along the coast of Cochin China against the monsoon, keeping the land close aboard to avoid the currents, when a flaw of wind, something in the nature of a " white squall," swept unexpectedly down a ravine.

It struck the ship with all sail set, and threw her instantly on her beam ends. Sheets and halyards were let fly, but for a few minutes the position was critical.

Fortunately the fore topmast went over the side, taking the main topgallant mast with it, and this enabled the ship to right herself somewhat and enabled the crew to get the main and mizzen topsails on the cap and the courses hauled up.

To enable this to be accomplished the anchor was let go, bringing the ship head to wind and assisting her to right herself—a manœuvre not often practised.

The danger was over in a few minutes, but it left much work to be done. The task of clearing the wreck, repairing rigging and fashioning new masts from the rough spars meant hard work for all hands for several days. And here the Greenland sailors proved their worth. They were used to mishaps of this nature cruising among the ice, amid the fierce winds of the Arctic. In fact, the excitement and the sudden heeling over of the ship seemed to stir their blood, and they tackled the ensuing work with energy and skill. So much so that practically everything was saved and all the wreckage got on board again.

Accustomed from childhood to the boisterous waves around their almost sea-girt home, the men could swim like sea-gulls. They dived among the wreckage, cutting away sails from yards, unreeving running-gear and getting wire backstays clear of the mastheads, whether above or below the water, in an astonishing way. Indeed, they appeared to revel in the work : there was no word of grumbling nor any sign of hanging back. Father gave his townsmen great credit for their behaviour and jokingly pointed out the contrast between it and their unmanageableness in fair weather.

Whalemen were a class of seafarers entirely different from all others. The ships they sailed in, the nature of their work, the conditions of their life on board ship were as different as possible from those of the

G

ordinary run of merchant vessel. Whaling and whale-men were in their hey-day when I was a boy, but since then have continuously declined in numbers and importance.

As a youngster I was often brought in contact with them. One of my most vivid recollections is that of the departure of the Aberdeen-Greenland whaling fleet in the year 1860. I fancy it was one of the last contingents which ever left that port for the Arctic on a sealing and whaling cruise.

By this time the once-important fleet (from that port) had been reduced to three vessels. It was composed of the very ancient, full-rigged ship *Pacific*, of about three hundred and fifty tons, and two brigs, the *Lady Franklin* and the *Sophia*, which, their names would seem to suggest, had been built for the purpose of searching for vestiges of the fate of the expedition which had set out to discover the North-West Passage under Sir John Franklin in 1845.

On the occasion on which I saw them set sail the crowd of seafaring folk on the north pier were discussing the chances of some of Franklin's expedition still being found alive, living with the Esquimaux in the neighbourhood of the Great Fish River; and this in spite of the fact that McClintock had lately returned with evidence that some at least of the members of the party had come to a fatal end.

Though the three ships that put to sea were only a poor remnant of the once-flourishing fleet which had annually departed from Aberdeen for Greenland or Davis Straits for perhaps a century previously, they still kept up in a minor degree the peculiar customs attending their departure.

For some days before they left the figureheads of all three ships had been adorned with fluttering ribbons. As they got under way the old tubs presented

a very quaint appearance. At the fore topgallant mastheads the " crow's nests " had been hoisted aloft; from the old-time wooden davits the whaleboats hung, and under the tops were slung a number of carcases of beef—soon to be frozen hard and so to keep for months. It was the fashion in which Greenlanders carried their perishable provisions; and it sometimes happened that a joint would be brought back in perfect condition from a voyage several months in duration. I remember a party once being regaled on board a Hull whaler on a joint of roast beef which had made the voyage to Davis Straits and back.

Festivities prevailed in the town for several days prior to the departure of the fleet. It carried the fortunes of not a few of those left behind; and should disaster overtake it, or a part of it, would result in a mournful echo ashore.

Just inside the point on which the Girdleness Lighthouse stands, on the south side of the entrance to Aberdeen Harbour, is a little bight named Greyhope Bay. At the time of which I speak it was memorable locally as the scene of the wreck of one of the whalers outward bound, a number of years before. This ship, the *Oscar*, having for some time been windbound in the Bay, attempted to make an offing and was becalmed. To avoid drifting ashore she came to an anchor in Greyhope Bay.

While she was still there a violent north easterly gale sprang up. There was no room for the *Oscar* to get under way, and her company were obliged to trust to their anchors. They dragged, and the vessel was driven ashore.

The mainmast, which had been cut away in the hope that it might fall and form a bridge between ship and land, unfortunately fell alongside. The vessel went to pieces under the eyes of the helpless watchers, and of the forty-four men on board only two were saved.

The tragedy was commemorated in a local ballad which began :

" I was on board the *Oscar*, a young and ardent dreamer :
    Between whose masts a garland hung, with pennons fluttering
        free;
    For every sailor's sweetheart contributed a streamer
    To bring luck to the whaler *Oscar* upon the frozen sea."

The reference in the second line was to the symbol of departure which was anciently hung aloft on all whale ships leaving Aberdeen. It took the form and name of a " garland " and was simply an iron hoop, covered in and decorated with ribbons of gay colours. In addition to being displayed on departure it was also hoisted on the 1st of May, by which date the ships were in Greenland and which was always kept as a holiday there.

On that day the " greenhorns," those members of the ship's company who were visiting Greenland for the first time, were initiated into the honourable fraternity of " blubber hunters " in much the same way as those on board a southern-going ship were introduced to Neptune on crossing the line.

The novice in northern waters, having first been blindfolded, was handed a speaking trumpet and ordered to hail the ship in a seamanlike manner. As soon as the poor wretch did so a nauseous and evil-smelling compound was poured into the wide end of the trumpet. It had ridiculous effects, and the victim was lucky who found that his christening rite had been performed with undiluted salt water. Thereafter he was shaved and ducked in the time-honoured fashion in vogue farther south.

Though I do not recollect having seen ships depart

from home displaying the garland, I have frequently
seen them return adorned in that manner.

In such cases the model of a fully-rigged ship was
suspended in the middle of the hoop, which was
hung aloft between the masts. When the vessel was
berthed the whole contrivance became the prize of the
first two boys who got on board and mounting, one the
fore and the other the main, reached the topgallant
mastheads and lowered the trophy on deck.   It was
a proud moment in a Peterhead boy's life when
he marched up the Broadgate carrying the coveted
emblem.

The ribbons with which each ship's figurehead was
profusely decorated were tied in place the Sunday
prior to sailing. Each crew vied with the others in
having the finest display of flags, and it was the custom
of the townsfolk on that day to walk round the harbour
and admire the various displays.   The ribbons and
other decorations had previously been collected at " the
Foy," an old-established merry-making held by the
crews of each ship a day or two before, to which the
wives and womenfolk of the mariners had been
invited.

As the Temperance movement gained force the good
people of Peterhead professed to be scandalized at the
quantity of liquor consumed at these ancient and
uproarious ceremonies of leave-taking. They were in
consequence gradually being displaced by " soirees,"
at which a minister was asked to preside and more
innocuous beverages than alcohol were served, much
to the disgust of the more conservative " blubber
hunters."

The change had come about by 1860 or soon after,
though the practice of decorating the " leddy," as the
figurehead was always called (even if it represented a
seal or a horse), and making the ships resplendent with

tar the Sunday before sailing was carried on for a number of years longer.

Though Aberdeen had declined, in 1860 Peterhead was at its height as a whaling port. In that year thirty-two vessels left for Greenland, all sailing-ships, and the largest number, I believe, that ever left on one occasion. Thereafter they quickly diminished, until by the seventies there were only two or three left. A few years later, by 1900 at latest, there was not one regular whaler belonging to Peterhead. The few that survived were sailing from Dundee, where the struggle was continued for some years longer. To-day the only ships that go regularly to the sealing are those of Newfoundland, and these only a remnant.

When I was a boy the sailing of the Greenland fleet was kept as a public holiday. It usually took a couple of days, the vessels only being able to leave the harbour when there was sufficient water to cross the bar. As fast as she could the little tug from Aberdeen would lug one of the bluff-bowed craft clear and scuttle back for another. The granite piers and protection walls were all the time fairly packed with spectators. As each ship was towed past the pierheads the crew, which would number from forty to sixty men, manned every point of vantage and gave the " farewell cheers " with tremendous effect. They were answered by hundreds, almost thousands, of voices from the shore. It was a stirring spectacle, a sight that once seen was never forgotten.

When it was all over and some 1,200 or 1,500 stalwart seamen had left the little seaport, Peterhead had the appearance of an almost deserted town and the lassies had good reason for singing : " The flowers of the forest are a' wede awa'."

It was a dangerous life the men led in the Arctic. The ships were not always drifting slowly among the

ice-fields; very often they were in open water outside
the pack and, in their anxiety to reach some favourable
position to continue the " hunt," their officers would
carry on sail till all was blue, in a manner worthy of
the crack tea-clippers. These tactics at times had
disastrous results, and whaling seamen had plenty of
bitter experience in clearing away wreckage and
repairing damage.

One of the best-known whaling skippers of the time
was Captain Robert Martin. " Oily Bob," as he was
called, had the reputation of a most enterprising man,
if not exactly a careful one. Once, with the object of
getting amongst the seals at the earliest possible
moment, he was working his ship along the edge of the
floe against strong breezes. As there was continuous
daylight at that season of the year old Bob was pushing
her for all she was worth. At length tired nature
demanded rest and after a long vigil he retired to his
" sleeping sack " below, leaving the mate in charge,
with strict orders that no sail was to be taken in without
his knowledge.

They were at the time carrying topgallant sails,
which was slightly more than was prudent, but the mate
simply replied, " Very good, sir," and let her rip.

The wind, however, increased momently, and with
the topgallant masts bending ominously, the officer
deemed it advisable to report progress. Captain Bob,
roused from his beauty sleep, did not realize, the sea
being comparatively smooth, the actual force of the
wind and replied sleepily : " What's the matter wi' ye,
Jamie? Ye ken I want to get tae wind'ard. . . .
Ye're no feared, are ye? "

Stung by the retort the mate returned on deck,
determined " to obey orders, if he broke owners." He
had not long to wait; a " fresh hand at the bellows "
sent the old packet down and down, until a couple of

her lee whaleboats were washed away. A rising blast, and the three topgallant masts went simultaneously, breaking short off at the topmast caps.

Down below went the mate and poked his head in at the skipper's door. "How's she doing, Jamie?" said his commander sleepily.

"Fine," said "Jamie" shortly, "the three topgallant masts are ower the side, and twa o' the boats is awa', *but I'm nae feared.*"

The story brings to mind the tale told of another skipper, whose brig on a certain night was head reaching under her two close-reefed topsails and jib. The night was dark but the moon was expected to rise at midnight, and like many another mariner, he had great faith in that luminary as a "cloud compeller," or, at least, as capable of moderating the power of the wind.

Shortly after the captain had retired, leaving the mate in charge, heavy clouds began to bank up to windward, and thinking it would be advisable to lay the brig to under her main topsail—"a close-reefed mitten with the thumb brailed up," as the sailors used to call it—the mate went below to inform the captain.

He found the latter insistent to hang on a bit longer, assuring the mate that "when the moon rises she'll soon scoff all that"—meaning the threatening clouds and the like.

The mate went back to his watch and soon the moon did appear, but, as it rose, so did the fierce blasts, and an extra heavy gust blew the two topsails clean out of the bolt ropes.

Again the mate made his report: "Moon has risen, sir."

"Ah, that's all right: she'll soon scoff this little lot."

" CHEAP JACK."

A noted Tea stevedore at Whampoa.

" Yes, sir; she's already scoffed the two topsails, and as I came down was looking damned hard at the jib."

From which it would appear that even " blubber hunters " have a tradition of carrying on.

CHAPTER XI

THERE's never a doubt that singing was always popular at sea, and a few remarks on shanties, which were at their prime in the sixties, may not be out of place here.

In its simplest form the shanty was just a grunt, given by one among a number of men labouring hard in order that the efforts of all might be given together and at the same moment. If that were the origin of the solo part the cries of encouragement given by the bosun or officer directing the work may be taken to be the beginning of the chorus. It has been asserted that shanties are a modern innovation, and though this may be true of individual songs, in a wider sense one may be pretty sure shanties are as old as sailors.

There is little doubt that from the beginning of things all seafaring folk sang songs in their ships when unmooring, hoisting sail or when engaged in similar operations. They would have a solo part and a short refrain, sung by all hands, calculated to time a pull in unison at fairly lengthy intervals. Such is the almost universal practice of seafarers of every race who handle sail or oar to-day.

I have often listened to the songs sung on the Chinese war-junks in Whampoa Reach as they hoisted their great matted sails. They were of the same nature as those sung in British ships when hoisting topsails or the like, but sung to much slower time. The singer or shantyman would drawl out some four or five syllables and, after a slight pause, the others would respond with not more than three. There was also an interval of quite thirty seconds between each stanza, to enable the men, as I suppose, to get their breath. These war-junks carried huge crews, and the strange wailing choruses would be sung by two or three hundred voices.

Whatever may have been the meaning of these Chinese shanties, I have no doubt they boast extreme antiquity. John Chinaman is not much given to change, either in the nature of the craft he sailed or in the songs he sang on board them. As a matter of fact, many Chinese junks still in existence and sea-going have been in service from time out of mind.

Junk builders are not progressive, and when a vessel showed signs of decay she was not destroyed, but repaired—as far as was necessary and no more. On one occasion she might get new topsides, some years later another keel or perhaps new lower bends. The original fabric was renewed piecemeal, until there was nothing left of the original junk and nothing, probably, of many subsequent renewals. Yet of course she went by her original name and gladdened the eyes of many generations of successive owners. And some of the shanties, one is inclined to think, that one heard on board such craft in Canton River may have been heard there in the days of Confucius.

No doubt the " sea cheers " which Sir Robert Lindsay heard on a Scottish ship in the Firth of Forth in the middle of the fifteenth century represented a stage in the development of shanties. " Pourbossa," " pulpela," " capuna " and the other words he gives may have been shanties in embryo, or they may have been in the nature of maledictions shouted not *by* the men, but *at* them, by the boatswain, to encourage them to gain a pawl in much the same way as more modern officers were wont to ejaculate, " Heave my hearties ! " " Heave and pawl ! " and the like.

Old-time sea-officers, one may be sure, no more cared to have the men work silently than they did when I was at sea. If no one among the crew seemed ready at halyards or braces to take the initiative himself, the officer in charge would do so, using such stock phrases as " Cheerly, lads ! " " Rouse him up," " The longer the lighter " and so on.

At the main sheet it would be " Oh, lug him a-lee ! "; at the main tack such a phrase as " Board him in the smoke, boys ! "; or, when setting a stunsail, " Boom end her ! " All these might be called " sea cheers."

A further stage would be reached quite naturally. The above operations are all instances of heavy, strenuous work, but when squaring in the yards as the wind " free'd " after a spell of head winds, the task would not be so laborious and the men themselves were likely to be in jovial mood. At such times the singer would be led to add variety to the usual " Ah-he-oh " of the hauling chant by chiming in with " Fair wind, boys; the Sydney (or other) girls have got hold of the towrope ! ", or, when making sail, " Spread her wings, now ! Bully breeze, boys ! give her the muslin ! "

In some such way, I think, shanties developed from the natural inclination of men to " sing out " when there was a heavy job in hand which called for concerted effort.

As an instance of the prevalence of " singing out " whenever possible I may say that when I first went to sea the orders, during the operation of " putting the ship about," were not ejaculated but chanted. They were enunciated with much the same musical emphasis

as the look-out-man would give the cry of " Land-o-oh ! " or " Sailo-o-oh ! " or the leadsman would report the depth of water from the chains.

My own father always gave the orders in this way. He had been trained in the small vessels, mostly brigs and barques, in the Mediterranean trade, whose skippers, probably following more ancient custom, were wont invariably to chant the orders in this way.

It gave the listening crew to believe the man in command was absorbed in the operation in hand, and struck a chord to which they were not slow to respond. To a sonorous " Let go and haulo-o-oh ! " they would run away with the braces and bring them through the leading blocks hand over hand, with a hearty response a dry curt order never obtained. Mediterranean traders carried scanty crews, and it was essential that each man be encouraged to pull his weight.

The masters of the larger Indiamen, however, brought up in a very different school, disdained such methods. They had powerful crews, so it did not much matter. I have sailed with a captain of this class, and when he rapped out " Main topsail haul ! " as though he were sick of the whole business, the crew responded likewise—mechanically and without enthusiasm. It is a small point, but it made a great difference in practice, and served to illustrate the well-understood value of a song.

All sorts of shipboard happenings, sailortown allusions and references to well-known mariners went to swell the content of the songs sung on board. A collection of such, could they be made, would form a forecastle commentary on much of our sea history.

That phrase, for instance, largely used when running away with the slack of a fore or main brace, " Roundee come squaree " would always evoke the reply " Makee a main yard for John Angletairee," in memory of that Portuguese shipwright who, having willy-nilly to repair some old worthy's spars, in Queen Elizabeth's days perhaps, demonstrated the method by which he intended to do it :

> " So roundee come squaree
> Me makee de main yard
> For John Angletairee."

On my first voyage to sea one of our A.B.'s was a bronzed and scarred old veteran who had seen much service on the Spanish Main among other places. In West Indian waters he had been concerned in ventures of a buccaneering and slave-trading nature, to which he sometimes alluded. Invariably, when we were setting a topmast stunsail, after the usual chant : " Boom end her, boys," he would chime in " —and look at the town." The phrase sounded meaningless to me, and I asked him what it meant. He said the words " look at the town " were those they always used when running across the Caribbean before the trades, and were passing by the towns on the mainland of South America or on the coast of Cuba.

I have already referred to the source of " Stormalong," and no doubt, in its origin, every one of the shanties and sea cheers had a peculiar and appropriate meaning.

Among the simplest of the shanties were the " tramp and go " choruses. One of the most popular was the rollicking :

> " Oh, hurroo, and up she rises,
>   Oh, hurroo, and up she rises,
>   Spread her wings to the bonnie breezes,
>   Early in the morning.
>
> What shall we do with the drunken sojer?
> What shall we do with the drunken sojer?
> Put him in the roundhouse till he's sober,
>   Early in the morning.

> What shall we do with the drunken sailor?
> What shall we do with the drunken sailor?
> Put him in the longboat and let him bale her,
>   Early in the morning."

That the song is ancient is indicated by the use of the word " roundhouse," which cumbersome addition to the poop or quarter-deck was unknown in the nineteenth century, so far as I am aware. It differed from the majority of shanties in that not only the soloist but all hands joined in the legend as well as the chorus. (I use the word " legend " in default of a better, to denote the song as distinct from the refrain.)

It was what was termed a " hand over hand " shanty, that is to say, one demanding a continuous pull, not a long drag at intervals. As it was impossible for a dozen or so men to get at the fall of the halyards in up and down pulling, the fall was rove through a leading block hooked to an eyebolt in the deck, and the bulk of the crowd tailed on abaft the block, and either kept hauling or walked away with it—" tramp and go."

The three verses I have quoted were all I ever heard sung on board a southern-going ship, but our north-countrymen added a couple of stanzas I have never heard elsewhere.

The first is interesting as recalling the days when Scottish brigs were engaged in the wine trade to Teneriffe, Madeira, and the Canaries. The Protestant composer probably found inspiration listening to the bells of the numerous monasteries in those places. His effort is realistic :

> " Ting-a-ling-ling for the Virgin Mary,
> Ting-a-ling-ling for the Virgin Mary,
> Ting-a-ling-ling, and that's all we caree,
>   Early in the morning."

The second, in these days of shanties' carefully bowdlerized popularity, is not for publication.

Another type of sea-song, and that among the oldest, was the bowline shanty.

When hauling aft a fore or main sheet the men would begin with the usual hauling chant : " Ho-ee-oh ! ee-oh-ho-oh ! " Not everyone, it should be said, could render this chant melodiously, and a good " singer-out " was a great acquisition to a watch. When the weight of the sail was becoming much heavier at each pull and little progress was being made, the mate or boatswain would give a hint (never quite an order) : " Sing-song, boys," or the shantyman would start on his own initiative. Then the men would mechanically cease hauling and wait for their cue, as indicated in the final word of the refrain. Thus the shantyman began :

> " Haul the bowline,
> The fore and main top bowline,"

whereupon the crew chipped in :

> " Haul the bowline,
> The bowline HAUL ! "

At the final " HAUL " all laid back together with a result hardly to be credited. A foot or more would be gained on a sheet as taut as an iron bar, which hitherto a watch tackle would hardly shift.

With a shanty of this description, where only one pull was given to each verse and, as a rule, not more than three pulls were required, there was little variation. There were two or three stock lines, each finishing with a word rhyming with " bowline "—" The captain is a-growlin'," " The ship she is a-rollin'," " Kitty is my darlin'," and similar doggerel.

Whatever may be the case with other kinds, I venture to think that bowline shanties at least are ancient. The " Complaynt of Scotland " has the words " Bouleena, bouleena," as well as the phrase, " Hale the Bowleen."

When we come to the " heaving " shanties one cannot be quite so sure. It is not clear to me how a shanty of the ordinary pattern could be sung at work at the primitive form of windlass. But in the poem above mentioned one verse at least seems to be descriptive of singing out while heaving up the anchor. " Vayra " seems to have affinity with " veering," and " hissa " with " hoist," while it is possible " capuna " comes from the old Scots verb " to coup," that is, to turn round or over, and may have had some connection with turning over the old barrel windlass by means of the bars.

In the Navy and in the early Indiamen the anchors were " got " by capstans instead of windlasses. The fact made shanties possible, and probably some singing took place. In merchantmen fitted with the ordinary type of windlass anything more than disconnected cries would be impossible. However, when windlasses began to be fitted with hand brakes and curved iron whelps were bolted on to the barrel, it became unnecessary to stop the work in order to fleet the cables, and a sustained song was capable of being developed. In some such way shantying may have come into its own. But I fancy that " self-fleeting whelps " did not come into fashion much before the Crimean War.

In the Indiamen the main capstan for anchor work was usually situated on the quarter-deck, or on the main deck abaft the main mast, and the cable was hove in by means of a " messenger," an endless rope or chain that is, of which one bight encircled the capstan while the other strained round a bollard in the fore part of the ship. An old song describing a ship's departure has it :

> " Oh, your messenger take to,
> Heave your anchor to the boo (bow),
> And we'll think on the girls
> When we're far, far away."

H

On starting to " up anchor," the cable was lashed at intervals to the messenger by means of temporary " stoppers," and relays of men were in attendance to " seize " on the stoppers and cast them off as required. I believe in some cases the spindle of the quarter-deck capstan extended to the deck below, and the messenger would travel round a " boss " thereon; and, possibly, capstan bars could be shipped into a boss on the spindle on the lower, or main, deck as well, so that two separate gangs of men could be employed.

As shanties were not allowed in the British Navy, at least in later days, and probably not encouraged in the Indiamen, some other kind of music had to be provided. We read that about the year 1623 Captain John Weddell, in the *Royal James*, had an organized " noyse " or band with him, though we get no account of the instruments used. No doubt in those days, as later, a fiddle was the favourite instrument.

At Bombay in 1853 my father in the new China clipper *Merse* lay near the *Vernon*, an ancient type of Blackwaller, discharging a general cargo from London. He used to watch the crew walking leisurely round her great capstan, slowly hoisting a bale at a time, and cheered (or lulled) by a fiddler perched on the capstan head. As late as 1861, the *Highflyer*, another of Green's, had a fiddler on her muster roll.

At the same time the presence of a fiddler on a ship's company was not proof positive that shanties were never sung in that ship. When the crew of the tea-clipper *Black Prince* were being signed on at Tower Hill Shipping Office in 1866, I and another lad were sent round among the knots of seamen standing about to try and secure a fiddler. We were at last successful in finding one by the name of " Yankee Ned " who guaranteed ability to play " The wind that shakes the barley," " Jack's the lad," and other lively airs. But,

✗ Septimus Cook Hawkins was an officer on board her.

as he ultimately came to sea without his fiddle, we never actually heard him. But shanties were not lacking and carried us through successfully.

Finally there were a number of so-called shanties, very popular during the last days of sailing-ships, such as " Blow, boys, blow, for Califor-ni-o " and " We're bound for the Rio Grande," which are obviously modern. But such songs are not really shanties at all, nor are they adapted to be sung by men who are labouring hard. The choruses are too long, and though they make rattling good songs, they are more suitable for a glee party. The shanties proper, always to be known by having a chorus of less syllables than the legend, culminated in such rousing old things as " Sally Brown," " Stormalong," and " We're all bound to go."

CHAPTER XII

NAURU OR PLEASANT ISLAND

THE traverses one made in a sailing-ship were very different from those of steamers nowadays. The winds then, of course, were the deciding factor. Coasts and islands in consequence usually considered very much out of the way were then on the ordinary track of vessels. Since the disappearance of clipper-ships many of them have again sunk into obscurity, but others have proved of commercial value or strategic importance and have taken their place in the world of overseas trade.

In the *Chaa-sze* and *Black Prince* I had become acquainted with most of the better- and many of the lesser-known routes of the East Indies and elsewhere, but one of the most out-of-the-way places I visited was in the *Norman Court* in 1871.

That was Nauru or Pleasant Island, lying almost on the Equator in the Pacific, remote and lonely between the island groups known collectively as Micronesia and Melanesia. I was chief mate of the *Norman Court* at the time; we were making a passage from London to Shanghai and racing against the well-known clipper *Sir Lancelot*, which had distinguished itself as having made the record passage home from Foochow to London with new teas in 1869. The *Sir Lancelot* had left London some twelve days before us, also for Shanghai, and as we had no hope of making up this time against such a flyer, our only chance was by taking a different route.

116

There were three routes (at this season of adverse monsoon) open for China-bound ships from Europe. One was by the Straits of Sunda—with a hard beat to windward up the China Sea. The second was by the Straits of Timor, thence through the Eastern Archipelago (to the north-west of Australia) and into the North Pacific by Gilolo or Dampier Straits, north-west of New Guinea, and thence north by the Loochoo Islands into the Yellow Sea and Shanghai. This saved the beat to windward, but was a much longer route than the first, and there was a chance of a calm spell about Timor.

The third route was of greater distance still and was not often adopted, though one was reasonably certain of fair winds (and quite enough of them) all the way from the Cape of Good Hope to Shanghai. This route was to circumnavigate Australia, either round the South Cape of Tasmania or through Bass Strait, between the latter island and Australia, thence via Norfolk Island, and, sailing north between the Fijis and New Hebrides in about 170 E., strike to the north-west by Pleasant Island. Having crossed the Equator, one sailed north of the Carolines and, passing through the Ladrones, fetched into Shanghai through the Loochoos.

We had adopted the " long trail " and had had good luck. We had had another famous clipper, the *Thermopylæ*, to try our mettle against in the first part of the passage. We had left the Downs on Christmas morning, 1870—our decks covered with snow; it was the year the Germans lay around the forts of Paris—and had a fine run down Channel. The *Thermopylæ* left the Downs on the 26th (she was bound for Melbourne) and came romping along with a fine north-easter. She was close on our heels before we got the benefit of the same good breeze and bowled away at our best speed.

From Madeira, which island we sighted on the eighth day from the Downs, we crossed the Equator nineteen days out, and passed the meridian off the Cape of Good Hope on 3rd of February—forty days from Deal, thirty-eight from the Lizard. The *Thermopylæ* crossed the line on the same day as ourselves, thus beating us by one day from the Downs.

But that was her luck on the run down Channel. When a little to the eastward of the Cape we sighted her again, but could not measure our paces together as it was late in the afternoon. We were running dead before a westerly wind with the after course furled, while she was steering a couple of points more southerly, thus bringing the wind on her starboard quarter. She crossed our stern, but on our bearings when night fell we had made about the same amount of easting. At any rate, the day that she rounded Cape Otway into Port Phillip, we rounded Cape Pillar on the south-west coast of Tasmania, on the 2nd of March, sixty-five days out from the Lizard.

This was very good, and had we been bound to Sydney we should in all probability have beaten the record, which was at that time sixty-nine days from Plymouth; but we had a long row to hoe yet. We sighted Norfolk Island on the 8th of March, and, as I have said, sighted Pleasant Island on the Equator on the 22nd of March.

We came upon the island suddenly. We had shaped a course for it as it proved that we should be in the latitude of it just about the time when it would be possible to get a good " sight " of the sun for longitude, but in those days one could never be quite sure of the chronometers. We had no ambition to have intercourse with the natives, as, according to the " Pacific Directory," these gentlemen did not bear a very good name. They had vague ideas of the sacredness of property. It was very seldom that any ships touched at the island save American whalers, who called occasionally to refresh their crews, keeping good watch and ward the while.

On the day in question I was roused from my forenoon sleep by the firing off of our regulation muskets—evidently the old man was preparing for action—and a boy brought a message for me to shake off dull sloth and get forward to take in the stunsails, as we were about to back the mainyard—to receive the " King of the Cannibal Islands," so the youth asserted.

As responsible officer in charge of some 1,500 tons of valuable cargo—a large portion of which was composed of eatables and drinkables, just the right sauce to accompany the tough old salts composing our crew should they be served up at the royal table—I did not view the captain's preparation with entire composure. But he laughed at my caution and asserted that he had had dealings with South Sea Islanders before I was born.

We were still some three or four miles to the southwestward of the island when our first visitor, in a smart whaleboat, lay right across our track, making it necessary for me to haul down the stunsails and lay the ship to. But I left myself a loophole of safety—by keeping the mainyard well on the square so that the ship's way would not be altogether deadened, and a touch on the wheel would set the clipper going through the water. The whaleboat came alongside, and the steersman, a villainous-looking, red-bearded white man, came on deck. The crew were some six or seven strapping Kanakas. They had a few very well-made coir mats, some coco-nuts, etc., for barter, and required in exchange some powder, tobacco and biscuits.

While their leader was below with the old man, bargaining and discussing a " four-finger " of rum, we noticed about half a dozen great canoes coming along, each of them being manned by about a dozen paddlers. Before the first canoe came alongside, the " Pirate," as we called him, was putting his acquisitions into the whaleboat. He seemed very satisfied with them, especially the flask of powder. As a matter of fact, as the captain had not seen the others approaching, the first comer had got the cream of what we could spare, and he seemed in a great hurry to get ashore with it. He had scored owing to his possession of more up-to-date transport. The whaleboat was a little beauty and had been obtained from an American whaler which had touched at the island.

One of the big canoes got alongside as he left, and he passed the time of day with the " boss " thereof, who proved to be another white man, hailing from another village somewhat farther to the west. This " boss " was a man of about sixty, answering to the name of Harris and known among the rest as " King " of Pleasant Island. He also was on the look-out for stores. He himself informed us that his brother had been Mayor of Plymouth, and from others we learnt that he had reached his present kingdom by way of Botany Bay or Norfolk Island. His had been a free passage out from England, the home authorities deeming that the Mother Country would be a happier place without him. However, he had given Norfolk Island the slip on board a whaler and so had reached Nauru. Possibly most of the other white men—of whom there were at least six on shore—had gone through the same experience.

As the red-bearded man in the whaleboat was pulling off, another canoe hooked on to our forerigging and sheered alongside. I had, as I said, kept the main topsail on the shiver, as I did not feel so confident about the good faith of these savages as my father did, and the ship was then ranging through the water at some four knots or so.

By the way in which the man in charge of the second canoe, a half-caste, was manœuvring, the " Pirate " realized there was some danger to his whaleboat. He roared out some orders in Kanaka, but, whatever they were, they could not be carried out owing to our way through the water. It was not quite clear how it happened, perhaps the head-rope of the canoe got under the bows of the whaleboat, but she heeled over and filled with water. When I looked over the side there she was floating astern, full to the gunwale, with the crew overside clinging on.

The " Pirate," with his red head showing above the boat's sternpost, was spouting salt water and profanity. When he had recovered breath sufficiently, he shook his fist at the half-caste and roared out : " Hold on, you something son of something else, wait till I get you ashore ! " I shivered to think what the poor man's fate might be : he looked desperately scared, and " Redhead " was a typical bully.

Yet there was some excuse for the " Pirate's " wrath—his biscuits, flour and flask of powder were all under water. The last would no doubt be the greatest loss. The crew soon managed to get into the whaleboat again. They bore down one side of the boat into the water until the other gunwale was a foot or so above the surface. Then they let go simultaneously and the boat righted quickly and evenly, and at the same time was freed of about six inches of water. Thereafter they scooped the water out with their hands until one man was able to get into the stern sheets and throw it out. In less than five minutes they had emptied their craft of water as of everything else, and then made sail for home—probably to make ready for revenge.

The half-caste turned out to be King Harris's

eldest son—there were about a hundred other princes we were told—and the pair seemed concerned about the " Pirate's " menaces.   The first question King Harris asked the captain when he came on board was : " What day of the week do you make it ? "   " Saturday," father replied.   " So I told them," rasped the King, " but the silly beggars would have it it was Sunday."   They had lost their reckoning and no ship had touched there for some time to put them right.

By this time the deck was fairly full of natives, mostly tall, strapping fellows.   They were really fine specimens of humanity, and each man carried a long knife stuck in a belt round the waist.   Each one of them had some little thing to barter, and was most anxious to obtain tobacco, old iron and bottles from the crew in exchange for their coco-nuts and trifling curios.   I did not like those long knives, though I was somewhat reassured by the presence of two English sailors.   They were decent-looking young fellows who had left an Australian barque and stayed on the island, where they had now been settled about eighteen months. They assured me that the natives did not contemplate mischief.   I had told off two or three apprentices and others to keep a kind of guard with muskets, and had served out cutlasses to the men, advising them to keep them out of sight, but they were not required, and everything went off smoothly.   The only memento I brought away from Nauru was a kind of wooden sword, the cutting part of which consisted of sharks' teeth tied on the blade with coir thread.

We offered the two Englishmen a passage to China should they wish to leave the island.   They declined with thanks, saying they were not tired of the life yet. They were both married, very much married, and one of them introduced me to one of his fathers-in-law. These white men lived at different villages, and were

convenient to the headmen in trading with whalers and
other passing ships. The two sailormen I spoke to said
they had nothing to do but amuse themselves, their
wives finding all necessary provisions. They said that
their side of the island, the south, was at war with
the other side, but this did not trouble the white men
apparently. The captain was quite delighted with the
appearance of the land, and old Harris cordially invited
him to come on ashore. Said the former : " Had I my
wife with me I think I might have had a stroll ashore,"
meaning had he been voyaging leisurely, as men do
who carry wives with them to sea. But old Harris
quite misunderstood him. " Oh, don't let that stop
you," said he, and gave us to understand that the
more influential of the inhabitants of Nauru had any
number of wives to spare.

However, I called our old man's remembrance to
the *Sir Lancelot*, and he told old Harris that he would
have to say good-bye. There had been one boat alongside manned entirely by " girls." These I sternly
forbade to come on board, placing a reluctant guard
with a couple of muskets to ensure obedience to my
edict. I thought it risky enough to have some forty
or fifty six-foot " Adams " knocking about our deck,
but I drew the line at " Eves " with their blandish-
ments to complicate matters. They tried hard to soften
my resolution and made faces at me, which, I believe,
were intended as love signals, but I hardened my heart.

Then an event happened which made me act
promptly. One of our men had had some dispute with
a huge native over some bartering. Knives were drawn
on both sides, and I think the native got an accidental
scratch. The carpenter, who was in charge of the
musketry, called my attention to this, and I determined
to end the " market." Old Harris was in his boat; so
I beckoned the man at the wheel to put the helm up,

and very soon the canoes were streaming astern and straining in their head-ropes. I gave all warning and cut away the women's boat first, and also put my knife quickly through the others' ropes. As our sails were filling, most of the Kanakas jumped overboard or into their boats—they did not trouble which—though some hung on board pleading for more bottles, biscuits or tobacco, not seeming to care that their canoes were drifting rapidly astern. The steward brought up a few remaining beer bottles, which were distributed, and the last of our visitors reluctantly left.

The ship was now trimmed on her course and travelling some eight knots. But these men did not worry; they held the biscuits or whatever else it was they had acquired high above their heads with one hand, while with the other they let themselves drop gently from the after bumpkins into the water. Then they gave a stroke to clear themselves of the eddies of the wake, and literally walked away after their canoes. They were breast-high clear of the water, holding their treasures dry, and paddling quite leisurely towards their friends. I did not observe any sharks about, and it is possible the long knives were carried for the benefit of those enemies.

We were just bending on our topmast stunsail when another canoe was sighted coming towards us as we rounded the west point of the island. The men in it waved furiously, and we steered towards them. It turned out to be a very small canoe with two white men in the stern and some livestock in the centre. The captain said : " These two poor devils look miserable; pull in the mainyard a bit and let them come alongside."

The occupants of the canoe in their turn came on board. They hailed from a different part of the island to our previous visitors, and were the folk with whom King Harris's subjects were at war. We gave them some stores and hauled their two ugly pigs on board. These latter were striped like tigers. The boatswain called my attention to one of the natives in this boat; I never saw such a huge man in my life. We could not estimate his height as he was crouching low, but he presented a smooth back like the side of a whale. I should say he measured between four and five feet across the shoulders, while his arms and thighs were of prodigious circumference. These two white men looked altogether more miserable than those from the south side of the island, and were evidently settled amongst a poorer tribe.

As soon as we had " Dennis " safely over the rail we filled away, and running up our stunsails (we carried topgallant and royal on fore and main), ringtail and " Jamie Green," we were once more on the track of the *Sir Lancelot*, having lost some precious hours and secured two animals which might, by courtesy, be called pigs, but which tasted more like shark. They had evidently been brought up on the sea beach.

We had also obtained a litter of black and white puppies in the course of barter; we were told they would be good " scoff " when stuffed with coco-nut and served up " à la sucking pig." However, as they looked like fox terriers we decided to rear them. They grew into great shambling dogs and arrant cowards, so having let them pass the critical period for roasting, we gave all save one decent burial. The survivor we presented to a Chinese comprador, making him swear by the " hook block " that he would keep it for our sakes until it died of old age, calculating that by that time it would have eaten him out of house and home. But we heard a few days later that the " Nauru pup " had figured as the principal dish at the obsequies of the said Chinaman's oldest wife. Whether the animal was sacrificed to do honour to the wife, or the wife was made away with to save the dog flesh, I cannot say.

So we left Nauru, for in 1871 no one, least of all King Harris himself, had any idea that Pleasant Island held £100,000,000 worth of phosphate rock.

CHAPTER XIII

PAGODA ANCHORAGE

THERE are few scenes that linger in my memory more vividly than the Pagoda Anchorage in Foochow River a day or two after the " new teas " market had opened, when the first flight of clippers was getting ready for sea.

The " opening of the market " was a feature peculiar to the Foochow tea trade. In the city of Foochow stocks of the first pickings from the tea-gardens in the interior had accumulated since early in May, but the Chinese merchants were slow in making up their minds to sell at prices acceptable to foreign buyers.

It was perhaps known from the outset that certain foreign " hongs "—that is, mercantile houses—would eventually purchase particular " chops " of tea. A " chop," I should say, was a number of boxes of the same make and quality of leaf, variable as to weight, but usually the product of one particular garden. " Chops " bearing a well-known name were bought year after year by the same foreign merchants, yet, even so, weeks were often spent in haggling. The price was slowly and reluctantly lowered by the Chinese merchant, the foreign buyer sitting tight. When it had been reduced sufficiently, some one of the more important firms was tempted to close, and " opened the market." Then the hurry began.

127

As soon as it became known that Jardine's, say, or some other well-known English firm had opened the market, all the rest of the merchants began to buy their favourite " chops " at proportionate prices.

Speed was the order of the day. Forty-eight hours or so were required to weigh and label the tea-chests, then each " hong " made all haste to load the same into the lighters which waited to convey the fragrant leaf from Foochow to the Pagoda Anchorage, a distance of about twelve miles.

It was a desideratum that the tea-chests, even though the tea was packed in air-tight leaden caskets inside the wooden cases, should be as little exposed to the air as possible. The " tea-chop," therefore, was contained in a long room, well-caulked to exclude air, much like an elongated, closed-in railway truck, placed on a low-lying craft instead of wheels. One mast arose from the small space of deck forward of the tea-room, on which there was only room to work one pair of sweeps and manipulate the windlass. Abaft the tea-room was another low deck, under which the crew of the vessel were accommodated.

Generally some three or four of the clippers with good records were chosen as " going ships," and combinations of shippers would concentrate on filling these, each clique endeavouring to have their ship first away. It was a keen contest; yet it was not always the ship which was considered the fastest which got away first. Much depended on the tonnage of the vessel and the status and influence of the agents concerned.

As a rule, each clipper in the running had already shipped a " ground chop," that is, a sufficient number of chests of tea of an inferior quality, carried at a slightly lower rate of freight than the new teas, and just sufficient to cover over the shingle ballast and so add protection to the aroma of the new crop.

It would usually happen that a dozen or more clippers would be lying ready, with holds swept and garnished, for two or three weeks perhaps, and never a lighter had come to the Anchorage to break the monotony of their wait. Then one day, or one night as likely as not, immediately after the opening of the market, the watchmen on the waiting ships would be kept on the *qui vive* by hearing the blowing of many conch shells and a distant din on the river. The hullaballoo would draw nearer and increase. It would be augmented by much shouting of weird cries and hails out of the darkness upstream, as the first " tea-chops " came down. The men on board the vessels kept up insistent sing-song calls, which represented, in the Chinese tongue, inquiries as to where they should anchor to be near the particular vessel for which their cargo was designed.

The method in vogue was to chant in a long-drawn-out wail the Chinese name of the " hong " which owned the tea. Thus Jardine Mathieson's employees would wail out unendingly in mournful cadence : " Ee-wo ! Ee-wo ! "; those of Turner and Company would snap back a discordant " Wha-kee ! Wha-kee ! " and others in like manner through a whole gamut of barks and whines.

Who it was that replied to them and directed them to their destinations I cannot say; certainly it was not members of the clippers' companies. I believe when they were expected Chinese rivermen were stationed in anchored boats in readiness to direct them. At all events, on the last of the ebb one would hear the rattle of chains as the anchors were let go all down the Reach. The crews of the various ships, disturbed in their night's rest, were able to retire again, wondering if any of the clustering craft anchored all round were for their own particular vessel.

I

When day dawned, hopes and fears would be set at rest. Round each of the two or three favourite ships some half-dozen or so lighters would be gathered. The rest of the fleet were out of luck and had to exercise patience.

Yet they had not long to wait. In about forty-eight hours the " Blue Peter " would be flying from the trucks of one or more of the fortunate ones, and the " tea-chops " would transfer their attentions to the ship next on turn.

The finest display of clippers that I ever remember seeing waiting for the market to open was in 1869. In that year no less than fifteen of these beauties, more like yachts than merchantmen, lay moored off the Pagoda, with holds ready, ballast levelled, ground chop stowed, waiting for the new teas. I do not suppose that in any other port in the world one could have seen such a fleet of beautiful craft as were assembled in the River Min on that occasion.

Among them were the *Thermopylæ, Leander, Windhover*, and *Kaisow*, all on their first trip; the *Spindrift* and *Lahloo* on their second; the proved and noted flyers *Sir Lancelot, Ariel, Taeping*, and *Serica*; as well as the somewhat older but still handsome vessels, *Black Prince, Falcon, Min, Flying Spur* and the little *Ziba*.

There they lay, their hulls actually radiant, as smooth and glossy as though they had been lacquered, with scarcely a seam visible. Their copper sheathing had been burnished by hand and carefully oiled, till it glittered brilliantly in the sunlight.

Aloft everything was " a-taunto "—yards freshly painted and squared to a hair's-breadth by lifts and braces; topmasts and topgallant masts bright and oiled; standing rigging freshly blackened, and all superfluous running gear unrove; and with snow-white awnings

with scalloped edges neatly stretched fore and aft of
each ship.

There was no great display of bunting except on
gala days. The agent's house-flag was flown at the
main as a guide to the " tea-chops "; while at the
mizen captains flew a pennant when they were aboard
their ships, which was hauled down man-o'-war fashion
as soon as " his highness " was over the gangway.

Everywhere the British Ensign waved supreme. It
was sometimes worn at the peak, but more often on a
flagstaff over the taffrail. To my mind, nothing set
off a tea-clipper having a continuous rail from the
knightheads to the stern, which was made conspicuous
by a brass moulding and was unbroken by high forecastle or poop, so much as the Red Ensign gracefully
hanging over the stern.

But it should be a full-sized ensign, not the
insignificant mockery of a thing which some masters
affected for economy's sake. At this time, when the
tea-clippers were at the height of their glory, we were
often complimented on the appearance of the *Norman
Court* as she lay at anchor in the River Min, and the
finishing touch to her good looks was the size of her
ensign and the angle of the staff from which it flew.
I happened once to be on board a steamer when the
merits of the various clippers in the Reach were
discussed. One man, an American, having no idea
who I was, remarked to me: " Ah! but that's the
pride of the river, the ship at the lower end of the
tier with the big flag over her stern." He alluded to
the *Norman Court* and, considering the splendid
clippers with which she was compared, I felt no small
pride that such was the generally accepted opinion.

On the other hand, the *Argonaut*, some three hundred
tons bigger than the *Norman Court*, with a full poop and
a long flagstaff, flew an ensign not much bigger than

a large pocket handkerchief. It completely spoilt the appearance of the ship and looked ridiculous, like a cock robin perched on an elephant.

Inboard the Clyde clippers were a perfect picture. Some of the later-built ones, such as the *Oberon* and the *Norman Court*, though not the *Cutty Sark*, had not only all their deck fittings such as houses, skylights, companions, pinrails round the masts, harness casks and the like, of solid teak, but their entire bulwarks as well, finished off with panellings and mouldings by cabinet-makers, in the same style and with the same care as the saloon bulkheads, though without the bird's eye maple insets.

This bright work, being skilfully treated with copal varnish, looked much like polished mahogany and formed a perfect contrast to the pitch pine decks, which were always kept holystoned pure white. Even the range of lockers for boatswain's stores under the low half-forecastle deck were finished off in the same elaborate style.

The earlier Clyde-built clippers were finished off in a slightly different way. Instead of varnished teak they had their bulwarks and the panels of their deck houses painted white or pale green, with gilt mouldings. This, though not so rich-looking and substantial as the later " mahogany " work, had its advantages on a dark night at sea, for one could see the ropes much better.

So much importance was attached to the appearance of the tea-clippers when in harbour that the *Ariel* and the *Titania*, built during the height of the tea-clipper epoch, had their bulwark panelling decorated with artistic designs in gilded work; though I am under the impression that they were " false " panels, only fitted when the ships were in port.

Thus in harbour, with the decks holystoned, the

braces laid on their gratings in neat " Flemish coils,"
and the superabundance of brass work brightly polished,
a tea-clipper of the period compared favourably with
the " saucy frigate " of Marryat's time, or indeed,
with a merchant vessel of any kind or period whatso-
ever. Had it been possible to keep them up to the
same high standard in smoky London or Liverpool as
it was with keen crews in the sunlight of Foochow,
their owners might easily have made an exhibition of
almost any one of them.

The high-water mark of excellence in appearance
was only possible for the few weeks when the clippers
were in port waiting for the new teas. But on such
occasions it was invariably the custom to give the
nicest attention to their looks down to the minutest
detail. Those ships that arrived later in the season
for the second crop, conformed no less rigorously to
the practice. Indeed, they had more time to do their
polishing and continued it through the period of loading, as they did not get the same quick dispatch the
" full-bloods " received. Sometimes, it is true, a
clipper arrived in Foochow to find her cargo awaiting
her, and then this " flummery " went by the board.
It did so, it must be confessed, much to the joy and
comfort of the sailormen, for whom it entailed much
hard and wearisome work, and who had no great
enthusiasm for it.

Leisurely and immaculate as the clippers looked, a
drastic change came over the appearance of the Reach
as soon as news arrived from Foochow that the market
was opened. It was then a matter of hours before the
ships chosen would be ready to sail. There was much
to be done; running gear to be rove and sails bent,
and everything put in order for a hasty departure to
sea. At the time of year when the new teas came
down—the month of May—north-easterly winds might

still be expected to carry the ship through the Formosa Channel, and stunsail booms had to be sent aloft in readiness. Moreover, as there were Consular orders in the port that as little work as possible should be done on board the ships during the heat of the day, it was customary for the " cracks " to start bending sail at four in the morning and endeavour to finish before gunfire at 8 a.m.

When two or more ships were getting ready in company, much rivalry ensued as to which ship, all of them starting together, should be the first to finish. To win it was necessary that any ship should have all plain sail bent to the yards and stays, with every roband passed; square sails furled with a neat " harbour stow "; " fore and afters " stowed in a cloth, and all hands below the sheerpoles. I forget what was the smartest time recorded, but any crew which had not finished before eight bells were considered a lubberly lot.

My liveliest recollection of the rivalry between the various ships was of a certain May morning in 1868, when we in the *Black Prince* were roused from sweet slumber on the booms by hearing the noisy crews of the *Ariel*, *Taeping* and *Sir Lancelot* as they started a sail-bending contest. It was admissible to make certain preparations on the previous evening, such as furling awnings, reeving gantlines and bending the sails on to them ready for swaying aloft at the appointed hour. At such times outsiders, who had spent half the night fighting mosquitoes, would have the privilege, not always appreciated, of hearing an immense variety of " stamp and go " choruses, as the sails were run up to their respective yards; all being sent aloft before the hands were ordered to " mount a-reevo ! "

At this period some of the tea-clipper captains, who

had no difficulty in obtaining the type of men they wanted, used to select their crews on racial principles. One fancied the " Blackwall " type of sailor; another preferred " men of colour " or negroes; while a third chose his crowd from among north-countrymen or lads of the Scottish breed; and yet another selected " blue noses " or Nova Scotiamen and seamen from the adjacent seaboard of North America.   On the particular occasion that impressed itself on my memory each of the three ships had a different type of seaman and their shanties varied accordingly.

Cockney seamen disdained primitive melodies like " Up she rises," and walked away with the gantlines to the tune of such music-hall ditties as :

> " That fair young girl,
> With her hair in curl,
> That works a sewing-machine,"

but these had not the ring and flavour about them of the older and more popular shanties.

A better result was obtained by that very ancient tune, said to have been an air to which Cæsar's Roman legions marched, with the rollicking chorus to which it was fitted :

> " We won't go home till morning,
> We won't go home till morning,
> We won't go home till morning,
> And then we won't go home."

This would be varied again by more modern marching songs, survivals, many of them, from the American Civil War, such as " John Brown's body lies a-mouldering in the grave " and " When we went marching through Georgia."

But a crew composed entirely of niggers gave, perhaps, the best entertainment. They sang with their whole hearts in the words and, at the same time, most

musically.   Many of their songs were reminiscent of the
Spanish Main.   I can still in fancy see " old Jackson "
with whom I was shipmates for three voyages, a magnificent specimen of a man, though as black as Satan,
rolling his eyes as, with a voice of thunder, he gave us
his favourite, " Running down with a press of sail " :

> " Running down to Cuba;
> Slinging the water over the rail,
> Running down to Cuba ";

then, with raised voice,

> " Oh, good Lord ! how de wind do blow
> Running down to Cuba !
> And our old man, he crack on so,
> Running down to Cuba ! "

Another shanty, a particular favourite with West
Indian negroes, seemed almost to refer to some forgotten
fight with Spaniards or buccaneers.   Somehow thus it
ran :

> SOLO : " Fire from the round top, fire from the bow,
> CHORUS : " Fire, O my lady, get down below ! "
> SOLO : " Fire from the main deck, fire from below,
> CHORUS : " Fire, O my lady, get down below ! "

After a couple of stanzas or so the shantyman would
make a supreme effort.   With a bellowing roar, passion
in his voice and the whites of his eyes showing, he
seemed to demand that his orders should be obeyed.
The crowd joined in, and the imperative command :

> " Fire, O my lady, get down below ! "

came in a frantic burst from a score of negro throats.
It was a song calculated to " raise the devil " and could
be heard all over the Reach.

Thus it went at Foochow, and Foochow in the sixties
was the premier port for the shipment of teas.   Though
it had been opened to foreign trade as far back as 1842,

WHAMPOA.
With East Indiamen in foreground.

for a number of years afterwards Canton, or rather
Whampoa, was the more important place. " Orange "
and " Flowery Pekoe," " Scented Capers " and other
choice teas were those for which the southern port was
famous.

It was to Whampoa that the *Chaa-sze* had gone on
her maiden trip, and there, while waiting with empty
holds for her cargo of tea, I recollect an amusing incident
that bore witness to the advantage of her " new fangle-
ments." Whilst she lay moored in the river, the great
Yankee clipper *Sea Serpent*, of some 1,300 odd tons, fell
athwart her hawse. Prompt action in easing the
" riding " cable so that the strain was taken equally
by both chains saved her from the worst consequences
of the mishap—that of parting from her moorings
and, together with the *Sea Serpent*, sweeping the
Reach.

But the towering American ship was foul of her
forward, and the *Chaa-sze's* crew of rugged whalemen
were given some idea of the autocratic ways of a real live
Yankee bucko-mate. Picturesquely attired, something
in the " cowboy " manner, with long jack boots, the
chief officer of the " *Sarpint* " raved about her decks
like a " hen on a hot griddle," emitting sulphurous
volleys of the latest American oaths.

The two ships were fast entangled forward, the rope
rigging of the *Sea Serpent* with the wire rigging of the
Chaa-sze. " Bucko " grew infuriated with his men as
they endeavoured to put matters right and roared out :
" Why the blankety blank don't you cut the double
blank things? they are only blank blank ropeyarns."
His harassed men attempted to do so, but their knives
made little impression on the *Chaa-sze's* wire, and in
their haste and confusion it was the *Serpent's* hemp
which got sliced up, to the blasphemous indignation of
the bucko mate. The " damned lime-juicer " fell clear

intact, while his own magnificent craft sheered off, bearing obvious tokens of the collision.

There were other features peculiar to the Canton River and one of the most noticeable, as it was one of the most detestable, was the number and impudence of its river-thieves.

These villains had a habit of visiting loading ships at night and stripping off a few sheets of their copper below the water-line. At one time this practice had become so common that a watch boat was stationed nightly ahead of each ship.

Even so, the thieves were not easily to be denied. Thwarted in their attempts to get alongside in their small one-man sampans, they eluded the watchman by their cunning and their almost amphibious qualities in the water. Canton had an enormous floating population, and every single member of it could swim like a duck.

To get at the coveted copper sheathing a Chinaman would float downstream with his nose just above water, his face concealed by a piece of matting, old basket or other rubbish. He carried with him a length of rope which he hooked on to the cable some distance beneath the surface, then, slacking himself away alongside the vessel, he would get to work on a selected piece of copper.

How the job of getting away with it was safely accomplished I am unable to say. Perhaps a sampan was ready some distance away to relieve the operator of his booty, perhaps the rogues adopted more elaborate methods. As a rule, a dark night was chosen and, when conditions were favourable to them, whole gangs worked together. It was no uncommon thing for vessels which had spent a week or two at Whampoa to be found to be on their arrival in London minus thirty or forty sheets of metal sheathing.

Sometimes, as I say, the theft was not discovered

till the vessel reached home; sometimes it came to light sooner. I remember on one occasion the *Mirage,* Captain Roberts, and the *Blackburn*, Captain Douglas, were lying abreast of each other in Whampoa Reach, half laden with tea. Strong winds, the result of a distant typhoon, had caused the two ships to heel over to a considerable extent and expose their port bilges. On the flood-tide the *Blackburn* was the weathermost ship and Captain Douglas noticed that several sheets of copper had been stripped from the bilge of the *Mirage*. He shouted across to attract Captain Roberts' attention, and pointed out the fact with, perhaps, a shade of amusement in his manner.

Roberts was intensely disgusted. The loss of the sheathing would make an appreciable difference to the speed of his ship, an all-important consideration for a tea-clipper. Worse still, the theft would expose the planking to the ravages of the " worm."

But at the turn of the tide when the relative positions of the two ships were reversed, human nature being what it is, he felt better. The bilge of the *Blackburn* proved to have been stripped with far more devastating thoroughness than that of the *Mirage*. His attitude of ostentatious merriment was the means he adopted of conveying the unpleasant information to Captain Douglas.

CHAPTER XIV

MASTER OF THE " NORMAN COURT "

THE honour of command came to me at an early age, and unexpectedly. I had served as chief mate for fifteen months under my father's command of the tea-clipper *Norman Court*, owned by Baring Brothers & Company of London. During that time my father had had several illnesses of short duration, the precise nature of which puzzled the doctors. At length his malady was diagnosed as " sprue," a complaint frequently met with in the East. In less than a year I am sorry to say it had proved fatal to him.

While we were in London, prior to sailing, father had enjoyed fairly good health, though there had been some question as to the propriety of his making another voyage. But finally he decided to do so, while I continued to act as mate. Fortunately I had been able to obtain my master's certificate during the last occasion we were at home.

So we sailed; and, encountering wretched weather running down Channel, father had a sudden attack of his strange complaint. It came upon him suddenly one night during a blinding snowstorm, with a hard south-easterly gale blowing. The ship was making about ten knots, and canvas had been reduced to afford some degree of safety should we come unexpectedly upon other craft during the thick drift. Father felt so ill he was compelled to leave the deck and go below—an absolutely unprecedented thing for him to do in heavy weather in the Channel. As a consequence I had my first taste of supreme control of a clipper under somewhat trying circumstances and was not sorry when daylight appeared and my vigil became easier.

During the night the captain had called for me and, giving me evidence of the serious nature of the trouble, asked my advice. What course should he take? Should he continue the voyage, or put into port in order that he might consult the owners and come to some arrangement? He gave me to understand he was considering my welfare. I might not like to sail under another master; and he had hoped, as he was part owner of the *Norman Court*, that after another successful voyage Baring Brothers might be content to hand over the command to me.

I was so alarmed at the change I saw in his appearance that I begged him not to think of me, but to make up his mind at once to stay at home, and I would take my chance under whatever master might be appointed.

He agreed to my advice, and as the wind had shifted into the southward and we were then standing in under the Start with Dartmouth under the lee, it was decided to put in there.

Luckily we picked up a pilot almost at once, and as he boarded us he said we could not have arrived at a more opportune moment. The tide was making and the shift of wind would enable us to negotiate the somewhat difficult entrance to Dartmouth Harbour without difficulty. We should soon be as snug, he said, as in " London Dock itself."

So it was: and before noon we were safely moored in the lovely landlocked basin. Father's paroxysm, meanwhile, had subsided and he felt a little embarrassed at the action we had taken. He said he felt ashamed to the north-west and the glass began to rise. I was well aware that

> " First rise after low
> Foretells a stronger blow,"

but I knew too the *Norman Court* was getting clear of the traffic-ridden waters of the Channel and repeated to myself the rhyme that Captain Robinson of *Fiery Cross* and *Sir Lancelot* fame was wont to impress upon his mates :

> " Starboard's green, and port is red,
> Carry on and go ahead ! "

so I cheerfully gave her the muslin.

Not all of it by any means. When we got the topgallant sails on her the *Norman Court* began to pay too close attention to the westerly sea still rolling up Channel, and I decided to let the canvas stand at that. The second mate, a good seaman, who had been in the ship the previous voyage, had the first watch.

About two bells it came on suddenly to pipe and we had to shorten sail. The outer jib had been set, and as the ship was diving heavily I thought to ease her by having the sail furled. The second mate went forward to see about it.

But there seemed to be a hitch somewhere and, hearing the violent shaking of canvas, I went forward to see what was wrong. To my disgust I found the inner jib shaking itself to pieces and everything in confusion forward. The wrong jib halyards had been let go by one of the many foreigners among the crew who were ignorant of English.

I shouted to the helmsman to keep the ship off the wind, to give them a chance to restore order, and hurried aft to look after her. The night was dark, and when I thought she had run off enough I gave the order to steady the helm.

The ship was still running off to port in spite of my frantic " Luff ! luff ! " I saw the man tugging at the wheel as if the helm had been put hard down and realized there was something wrong. I rushed aft. The helmsman, another foreigner, was straining at the wheel and jabbering excitedly, though what about I had not the faintest idea. Fortunately I guessed.

Owing to the slimness of our patent steering screw we used to keep relieving tackles ready to hook on to the tiller should the screw suddenly snap. These had been hooked on but left slack, and one of the blocks had jammed between deck and tiller.

Of course, I cleared the obstruction instantly, but it was too late. The ship had answered to her starboard helm until she had brought the sea nearly dead astern, and the wind broad on the port quarter, so she was taken by the lee and all aback. It was a most dangerous position for a vessel with a fine run aft and a low taffrail, with a heavy sea running. It was commonly said that some of the tea-clippers, notably the *Ariel* and *Titania*, in consequence of their excessively lean counters, would move as fast astern as they would ahead ; and though the *Norman Court* had certainly better bearings aft than these two ships, yet she was hardly behind them when it came to retrograde sailing.

I was more chagrined over the matter than alarmed, for it looked such a lubberly thing to have done, yet the risk was by no means negligible. If the bobstay, or one of the fore and aft stays parted, we were likely to be dismasted. So it was " let go the topsail halyards " and tumble out all hands. I set the watch brailing the spanker in, easing up the fore and main tacks and sheets, while gathering up the clew garnets and buntlines. When the other watch appeared on deck I set all hands to lug the head yards round and

K

I heard the roar of our cable rattling through the hawsepipe. The pilot had anchored!

I thought it meant good-bye to the ship. Confound the Chinaman! what had he disobeyed orders for? Our stern began to swing rapidly towards the rocky shore, and it seemed impossible for the ship to swing clear. All I could do was to give orders to " hold on every inch " and wait breathlessly for the devastating impact between our stern and the rock-face.

Then the unexpected happened. The same thing has been known to occur before, in Magellan Straits and elsewhere where the tides are very strong, and to save ships from disaster, plucking them, as it were, from the very jaws of doom. The very violence of the tide, rushing furiously between ship and shore, forced the vessel towards mid-channel at the moment she was about to strike.

It was a matter of inches, for, as our stern swung round, I could have jumped ashore. But the water was deep up to the actual rock-face and we swung clear, touching nothing. It was an almost miraculous escape.

As soon as the ship straightened up we tripped the anchor and drifted into shallower water outside, where we anchored again. A brisk southerly breeze sprang up that evening and enabled us to round Green Island (outside, after all), and bring up near the shipping.

The pilot was abjectly apologetic. He had, so he said, lost his head. It may have been so, or it may not. A wreck is always a godsend to Chinese fishermen, and ours may have been playing Providence when he let go the anchor.

A friend experienced in Chinese navigation, to whom I recounted the incident, whistled at my credulity in trusting to a Chinese pilot. I understood afterwards. Such men, fishermen, were often rascals. Some years later I myself had an instance of barefaced treachery on the part of one of them when navigating the *Norman Court* into the Yangtze River.

Yet a third instance of some unkind influence at work, on this my first voyage in command, occurred on the homeward passage.

We left Foochow on August 4th, and made a fair passage down the China Sea. We ran into a number of very violent squalls, almost tornadoes, on the way down, which we escaped from with no more damage than the loss of some canvas. The last was the worst: at one time it looked as though it would leave us without our topmasts.

We had reached nearly to the Equator, and one evening were standing in to the Borneo coast, being about ten miles off land. It was my intention to get well inshore to have the benefit of the breeze blowing off the land in the early morning. Such was the general practice of tea-clipper commanders, who sailed close in the endeavour to get a good send-off in their reach for Gaspar Straits.

The night was clear, but about eight bells in the second dog watch I noticed vivid flashes of lightning low down on the western horizon.

There was not a cloud to be seen, and it made me suspicious. To the astonishment of Mr. Brummell, I decided to tack to the westward to get a good offing in case this was another tornado brewing. The wind had fallen very light: we were scarcely making more than three knots with everything set.

Nothing happened. I stayed on deck all night, but the sky kept clear, though the strange lightning still forked out at intervals. When the mate came on deck again he smiled to see me still keeping my vigil. He thought nothing of it, and as daylight

CHAPTER XV

HANDLING A TEA-CLIPPER

IT was not every shipmaster who cared to have the handling of an up-to-date tea-clipper of the sixties. The commander of one of those tender beauties had to be continually on his guard against squalls and sudden changes of weather. Not for him the " take it easy " attitude of other shipmasters through spells of fine weather or in the region of the steady trades. Not even when the ship had been snugged down under low sail, and the more fortunate man felt he deserved and could legitimately take rest, was the tea-clipper man free from the obsession that he must crowd sail on his ship whenever the wind showed the least sign of abating. He had a China clipper under his charge, and she must never be allowed to lag. Her white wings were intended to be spread to the breeze, and anxieties were meant to be undertaken and overcome.

There was an old forecastle song, a great favourite of the shellbacks of my boyhood days, which illustrates this. After describing the operation of carrying on till the last moment, and the subsequent reefing of topsails, on board a New York packet-ship, whose officers had no other object than to make a speedy passage, the singer portrays the anxiety of the skipper to keep his ship going :

" In the very next watch
   There being a lull,
   Old Davey comes forward
   And roars like a bull :
' Come shake out those reefs, boys,
   More sail we must show,
   She's a flash Yankee packet—
   Oh, Lord, let her go! ' "

And the packets were not more hardly driven than the cracks of the China trade. It must also be borne in mind that a tea-clipper of 800 tons register would have spars equal in dimensions to those of an ordinary merchant-ship of 1,100 or 1,200 tons. Of course, she might be manned in proportion; but again she might not. Besides, the clipper was infinitely more lively in a seaway than the lumbering Indiaman of the period.

I have known a shipmaster of experience, who, one would have judged, would have been the last man in the world to show anything like the white feather, to get into quite a panicky condition during his first introduction to the quick motions of a new tea-clipper, as she faced a short head sea with a whole-sail breeze.

He was aware he was expected to make a smart passage and did not like to order sail to be reduced; which, indeed, there was really no need to do. So there he stood, clasping the weather-rail of the half-poop with one hand, and at every 'scend of the ship into the head sea lowering his body in unison and actually groaning. At last the ordeal became too much for him, and in came the royals and the rest of the lighter canvas.

As an instance of the lively motions of the same vessel, the *Black Prince*, I might say that on one occasion, while beating up the China Sea against the north-east monsoon, the men were sent aloft to paint the yards. The weather was fine, simply a fresh breeze and short head sea, yet several of these men, seasoned A.B.'s, were seasick, owing to the lively motions of the vessel. Those on the topgallant yards would be violently jerked through an arc of about sixty degrees every few seconds, then back again, and so on, *ad infinitum*.

Those who, like myself, had been " dragged up " in the tea-clippers were accustomed to their vagaries, though, candidly, we did not appreciate them " for a' that."

The earlier China clippers were built, probably under a mistaken notion, with a minimum of beam to length. The idea was to ensure a comparatively high speed in the light winds of the China Sea. In the golden age of tea-clipper history the new tea crop was shipped as early as May, when the monsoons were at the change and much light weather was to be expected.

As a consequence they were all on the tender side; given to lay over at a fearsome angle even with moderate winds, and in variable weather demanding to be handled with the care and attention required to be given to any other thoroughbred. When caught by a sudden squall under a spread of sail it was no use treating them in the ordinary manner. When passing the Board of Trade examinations, it is true, the candidate, asked what he would do in such a case, was expected to answer he would " get the ship before the wind." If he answered otherwise, woe betide him! He stood a good chance of being plucked. But all tea-clipper men knew better.

" Luff her up and shake it out of her," was the order, and heaven help the timid man who, in the middle of a squall, put his helm up and tried to run before it, as was the usual manœuvre in old-fashioned ships.

The full-blooded clipper resented such treatment; as she fell off the wind a couple of points, she gathered way, and with her sharply braced-up yards taking the

weight of the wind at a right angle, would lay down
to it until her fair leads were almost in the water, and
the helm refused to act. Almost on her beam ends,
she tore thus through the water, and would not budge
a point off the wind until the squall eased and she
became more upright again.

It was little use letting go topsail-halyards and the
like. At the angle at which the vessel lay, the yards
would not leave the mastheads, and the men were
hardly able to get about the deck. The unfortunate
commander, finding himself in this predicament, had
to keep his head as best he could, until the squall blew
over or his canvas blew out of the boltropes. Or, as
once happened to Captain Robert Deas, one of the old
school, the bobstay parted and away went his masts.

I had sailed with " Bobbie," and though he was
far from being a sail-carrier, he was by no means
nervous in other ways. He clung to the weather-rail,
his pipe between his lips, all through the ordeal, never
saying a word. Possibly he thought shouting was no
use when action could not follow.

It certainly was an ordeal, for to feel a ship going
over in this way until her lee rail was level with the
water, and one had a growing impression she was not
going to stop at that, was anything but soothing to
the nerves. But the experienced clipper master knew
better than to let this happen.

It was Captain Deas who was in command of the
new supreme clipper *Titania*, just " off the stocks," in
a manner of speaking, when she was dismasted near
the Equator outward bound on her first voyage. I can
picture the scene, as I well knew " Bobbie's " tactics
when I was in the *Reigate* with him—it was always
" up helm " in a squall. But what was good policy
in an iron ship of 1,100 tons, with somewhat full lines
below the waterline, was quite the reverse in a yacht

like the *Titania* of something less than 850 tons, yet
with a greater spread of canvas than the larger vessel.

The mate of the *Titania*, one Duncan, a man of
great experience in tea-clippers, who had been mate of
the *Ariel* and others, told me the story. He said he
quite expected disaster when he heard the order given;
yet he well knew Deas was not the man to brook inter-
ference with his orders, even if Duncan had thought it
politic to suggest anything at such a crisis.

The final catastrophe occurred through the parting
of the bobstay. Then the fore topmast went over the
side, taking the head of the foremast with it, and as
a consequence the main followed suit. I think I
recollect him saying she was left with nothing but the
mizen and the damaged fore and main lower masts.

As a matter of course, the master who elected, when
negotiating a squall, to luff his ship up into the wind
until the sails were shaking, had no sinecure while the
squall lasted. He could clew his lighter sails up and
let the topsail yards rattle down on the caps if he
desired, though of course the idea of " shaking her
up " was to obviate the necessity of reducing sail, and
consequent loss of time until things were normal again.

But to attain this, the skipper had to be constantly
" conning " the ship, so that she should not lose way
altogether and be taken aback, when the fat would be
in the fire with a vengeance.

Should he decide to keep the ship " off the wind,"
which could be done easily enough if the operation were
begun in time, he would have nothing to do as the ship
spoomed away before the squall. At the same time
he would have lost a number of miles of distance made
good, which was clean against the traditions of clipper-
sailing.

I have known masters who for many hours at a
time kept conning the ship through vicious and long-

continued squalls, keeping their canvas set and all ready to take advantage of the lulls. It was keen work, and occasionally a sail might be split, but it was how clippers were sailed.

On the other hand, the man who ran his ship off the wind was generally too nervous or too indolent to bring her to the wind again until he had reduced sail.

Very often the wind shifted a point or so during a squall. In such cases there was great danger of the ship being taken aback during the luffing-up process, and that was a point to be considered. Again, the wind might " free " a couple of points, which would lay the clipper on her broadside, but a spoke or two of lee helm would speedily bring her to the wind, though any amount of weather helm would not send her off it.

The man of grit would luff her up and con her for an indefinite time. The man who was lacking in nerve and self-control at moments of crisis was tempted to bawl " Hard up! " and " Let go! "—this, that, and the other thing until everything was in confusion. It was, as I say, the master who counted at such moments.

Our captain in the *Black Prince* had no love for conning his ship through squalls, and always deemed discretion the better part of valour. He usually kept her off the wind before the squall materialized. It was at a great expense of distance, of course, but Captain Inglis cared little for that. He had never won a race, except with his tongue, in his life, though from 1863 to 1866 he was in command of a clipper equal to the best of them. And he never would have won one, had he lived to be as old as Methuselah.

He was a good fellow though, and took life easily. He was fond of chaffing his officers on occasion. One voyage we had an elderly veteran as chief mate, a Scotsman, who had himself been master of one of the large Western Ocean timber-droghers. He was in consequence somewhat privileged, and had been heard to make sarcastic remarks anent his superior's easy-going methods.

Yet they remained good friends, and Captain Inglis took his revenge by ridiculing his mate's tales of former prowess.

One day, as a squall was brewing to windward, the skipper called to the mate : " Here, Mr. Davey, I am going below and will leave you to deal with this one."

" Aye, aye, sir," replied the redoubtable Davey, " I'll look after her."

He issued certain orders, and then, with one hand on the weather-rail, and after giving a stern glance round to see all hands were at their appointed stations, he calmly awaited the event. The watch looked on, expecting to see an exhibition of supreme seamanship, for we had all heard tales of great deeds done when he had been in command himself of the old *Clutha*.

Suddenly the squall swept down on us, and there was more weight in it than anyone had expected. The ship heeled over to the blast, and for a few brief seconds Davey fairly gasped.

Then, when he regained his breath, he emitted a gulp and a roar which stood for " Hard up, hard up ! " He had one arm free, and that and one leg he revolved vigorously, in time with the words, to emphasize the need of immediate obedience to his orders. The helmsman obeyed, and, turning to the men, Davey spluttered hectic appeals to " Leggo ! LEGGO ! "— practically everything.

By a stroke of good fortune the ship obeyed her helm on this occasion and no damage accrued. Then the captain made his appearance and surveyed the scene of confusion aloft. He could hardly refrain from laughing, but he turned a serious face to the mate.

" Good heavens ! Mr. Davey, what has happened ? What's the matter aloft ? "

Poor Davey, who had a little recovered his breath and equanimity, looked exceedingly crestfallen and muttered something about " Damned heavy squall, sir."

He never again dared to criticize the captain, who often teased him by asking how, on such and such an occasion, the old *Clutha* would have behaved. And forward, for a long time afterwards, the favourite amusement of the wags was to mimic Davey's frantic yells and imitate his limbs revolving like a windmill, in his eagerness to lend point to his words—" Hard up ! " " Hard up ! "

CHAPTER XVI

PIRACY was very rife round about Hong-Kong in the early sixties. The marauding fleets of Malay proas were becoming a thing of the past by that date, but not so the junks of Chinese pirates. Some of their fleets had been destroyed and their fortified refuges in the neighbourhood of Mirs Bay rendered useless by the British gunboats, but the scattered " pelongs " found they could ply their trade just as well, and in a more up-to-date manner, under the shelter of the British Ensign in the settlement of Victoria (Hong-Kong).

Out of sight in the native quarters about West Point, near that city, and among the " stews " of Endicott Lane and adjacent alleys, they were handy for obtaining first-hand information as to vessels with specie on board, either leaving or expected at the port.

About the same time as the *Chaa-sze* arrived in Hong-Kong, in 1862, the *Veronica*, one of Brockle-bank's ships, came in. She had narrowly escaped being taken by pirates, and I still have a letter from a friend of mine on board describing the affair. I quote it as a description typical of such a happening.

" We left the Thames in January, 1862," he wrote, " and arrived off the pilot ground, fifty miles from Hong-Kong, on the hundred and forty-eighth day out.

160

We picked up a pilot about 7 p.m., and at 8.30 p.m. I was lying down under the spars, it being my watch below. Suddenly I was startled by the Chinese pilot exclaiming : ' Captain, one pirate come; suppose he come on board, he kill.'

" The next thing I heard was the captain calling to the steward to hand up a rifle (one of the old flint-locks). These were ranged round the mizen mast. The steward passed the rifle through the skylight, and Captain Douglas let fly at the pirate. As the ball passed through his mainsail, the pirate immediately turned and ran away from us. (Arrant cowards, they rarely attacked if they lost the advantage of surprise.) He was only two hundred yards off; it was a moonlight night, and I saw all that happened.

" Our pilot supposed there would be about two hundred pirates on board, and had they boarded us and set fire to the ship great damage would have been done. You can imagine the explosion, as we were loaded with shot and shell for the Government.

" As soon as we arrived in Hong-Kong we reported the case, and the Government sent out a steam gunboat in pursuit. When she came back the authorities told us that twenty-two pirates would be hanged from the bough of a tree, not more than four hundred yards from where we lay at anchor.

" Sure enough, next day, when all the ships' bells were ringing noon, up went the first pirate (' Oh, hurroo, and up she rises ! '), and as fast as they could be lowered down the noose was put round the neck of the next, till the whole lot were hanged."

Never a year passed but several cases of piracy, attempted or accomplished, were recorded in Chinese waters.

In 1865 the tea-clipper *Childers* was sadly pillaged

L

when she got ashore outside Foochow. I have no particulars of that affair, but from an eye-witness who was shipmates with me in the *Black Prince*, I heard something of what happened when the *Young Lochinvar* (also bound to Foochow for new teas) met her fate in the following year and within a few miles of where the " ribs and trucks " of the *Childers* still decorated the sands. It was near daylight on a misty morning when the former clipper came to grief, just as a fleet of fishing junks were issuing forth to their daily business.

There was little wind, and one can imagine the delight of the poor fishers when they saw a handsome " three piecey bamboo," copper sheathed, with all her canvas set, hard and fast on their native rocks. It must have been considered a direct gift of the gods. The first of the boats that came alongside were allowed to enter as a " salvage corps," but as the mist cleared and dozens of junks closed with the ship, it soon became evident that salvage was out of the question, and menacing hints were made to the people on board to get into their boats and " hop it." At all events this was what was done, and the crews got safely away and were picked up later by a pilot boat.

By the time they got clear, the fishermen (pirates were too harsh a term) were swarming aloft cutting the sails from the yards, unreeving the running gear, and shifting everything movable. Boats clustering round the sides were getting laden with fragments of " yellow metal," stripped off and rolled up as the work proceeded. The ship being in ballast allowed the " salvagors " to manipulate three or four strakes of copper sheathing. The only cargo on board was 100 tons of pig lead, for which there was much demand at Foochow for lining the tea-chests. The pigs, each weighing 2 cwts. or more, were too weighty to be hoisted on deck without rigging some kind of purchase, so " Ah-sin " possessed himself of cold chisels and mallets, and hacked them into pieces more easily handled.

As the man who gave me the account said, when he got into one of the boats, he was amused to see a party hauling the " made-up " sails from the locker. As part of a sail emerged, and it was found to be jammed below, the Chinamen would not wait to clear it. They simply cut it off short, stowed away what they had got, and laid hold of another sail, the first that came handy —such eager helpers were they to lighten the ship. Reinforcements were still arriving as the crew pulled away—" the eagles " were flocking to " the carcase " —and probably by the time any assistance could be sent from Foochow, and nothing less than a gunboat would be of any use, the *Young Lochinvar* would be stripped to a gantline, and all perishable and other goods entirely " salved." She became a total wreck, and probably the natives had every particle of her in time, and I have no doubt the reigning mandarin had his tithes of the spoil.

In 1865 we passed an American ship which had stranded and capsized near the Mingan Pass, Foochow River, a day or two previously. Her bilges were black with a line of " salvage " men stripping her copper off sheet by sheet as the tide receded. Her masts were resting on the river bank, so possibly the local ploughmen claimed them. Again in 1874 the steamer *Canton*, laden with tea, silk and Japanese curios, struck on the Min Reef, a mile or two from the entrance to Foochow river. We, in the *Norman Court*, passed her as we entered the Min two or three days later. She was then surrounded by some fair-sized junks and many of the smaller fry. Some armed assistance had been sent by the Customs from Pagoda Anchorage, but the captain of the tow-boat which had conveyed the guard said the Chinese were too many for them, and much plundering (all under the pretence of salvage) was going on.

But all this was suddenly put an end to, as on the following day a typhoon passed along the Formosa Channel, and when it was over the *Canton* had almost disappeared. When we passed down, tea laden, some ten days later, there was little left of her above water.

We had a Chinese pilot on that trip (a good pilot, too), and, as customary, he made the officers a " cumsha." This was brought on board at Sharp Peak, a bulky package tied up in matting. He was mysterious as to the contents—" on'y a litty tea, velly good." When we got to sea and removed the outside cover we read, to our horror, the legend :

" Finest Souchong, via Suez Canal, per s.s. *Canton*."

It reached London all right, but by way of the Cape. A full chest, 100 lbs., of the finest new tea could not be wasted—at least our mates thought so.

These were the deeds of the Northern Chinaman; his southern brother used more drastic methods. " Piratical blood," indeed, has been said to be peculiar to the Southern Chinese. It was so in a special sense; in fact, I cannot call to mind any case of murderous piracy north of Amoy. There were plenty of thieves amongst the seafaring population all along the China coast, but none were so bloodthirsty as the Cantonese and their neighbours. These sought their prey where it might be found, and did not wait for the gods to send it to them altogether.

One of the most tragic acts of piracy that came under my notice happened in 1863, but was not revealed until 1864-1865. I had been in London in 1863, and was much interested in the homeward-bound list of ships from China, my father's ship being one of the fleet. I noted one name, the *Cumana* I think it was, which had left Hong-Kong in January and, though it was now autumn, had not arrived in London. Her name was still on the list when I sailed in December. Shortly after that she was posted as missing, and later again " Lost with all hands."

Though the matter had almost passed from my mind in 1865, in Hong-Kong in that year I heard more about it.

Some eighteen months after the *Cumana*, as we will call her, had left Hong-Kong, a certain shipmaster, prowling about the shady shops in Endicott Lane, where ships' stores were often to be had cheap and no questions asked, was offered a ship's chronometer, which he purchased. As it had stopped he took it to the only chronometer man in Hong-Kong—Falconer's, if I remember rightly—to be examined. A day or two later Falconer sent for the purchaser and requested to know how he had come by it. I presume this was revealed and the reason for such inquiry asked. " Well," said Falconer, " this watch was overhauled by me and put on board the *Cumana*, which was never heard of." The number was in the books of the firm.

The police were then put on the track, the shop-keeper's premises searched, resulting in other articles being found which could be traced to the *Cumana*; and so the mystery was revealed as to where the watch was obtained. Several arrests were made, and the following story told in court.

It transpired that the *Cumana*, leaving Hong-Kong late in the day, had anchored for the night outside the Lyee-moon Pass, and was well out of sight of either town or shipping, and not more than seven or eight miles distant, but in a very suspicious neighbourhood not far from the mouth of Deep Bay. With perhaps only one man keeping anchor watch, she was suddenly boarded by a gang of ruffians, the crew killed or driven below, the ship plundered, fired and sunk. It may seem incredible that this could be carried out so near an anchorage like Hong-Kong, but even if the fire had been noticed in that locality it would be thought to be a junk burning. The vessel was laden with cassia (Chinese cinnamon), and would burn like matchwood. I forget how many were executed for this affair, but to be sure a goodly number for the sake of example. Whether all were culprits or not it is difficult to say, as the filial instinct is (or was) so strong amongst the Chinese, that a rich offender had little difficulty in getting a substitute to swing for him, so long as a fair sum of money might be secured to the aged parents of the latter.

Turning from the pirate proper (who was not ashamed of his calling, but took the chance of being beheaded or strung up, should the fortune of war so determine) there were other aspects of the "tainted blood" of the Southern Chinese. I have already said something about their skill as river thieves, and the art, worthy of a better cause, they displayed in stripping ships of their copper sheathing when anchored in Canton River. But that by no means exhausted their delinquencies; it entered into all their dealings with "foreign devils."

The cunning and perseverance shown by the Chinese tally clerks of Hong-Kong in getting away with a package of cargo when a mate showed any carelessness in making his account of the goods delivered into lighters alongside, was worthy of admiration. Those same clerks, sent by the different lighterage companies, were usually a most polite and suave lot. Deceived by their bland and child-like smiles, one would have said "butter would not melt in their mouths." As a matter of fact, they were as artful as a wagon-load of monkeys, and never failed to take advantage of the slightest omission or oversight on the part of the officer who might be taking tally for the ship.

Many claims for shortages could in no ways be traced, and the ship had to pay, but I have in mind two cases of bare-faced attempted robbery which showed that the whole crew of the lighter were in the swim, and doubtless shared the plunder with the clerk and captain.

In 1868, while discharging general cargo from the *Black Prince* in Hong-Kong, our own agents, Turner and Company, had employed a lighterage company to take delivery of their consignments. Amongst them was a parcel of the largest-sized Manchester bales, containing a peculiar brand of cotton yarn—some fifty bales.

As part of these were being delivered into a craft, the Chinese clerk standing by the mate, marking the number of each bale simultaneously with the mate as it was lowered over the side, saw the latter had omitted to enter a certain number, though, of course, this was not determined until too late. On the ship being finally discharged, Turner and Company applied for a certain bale (No. 345, I think) which could not be found in the ship nor in Hook's " go-down " (warehouse).

Apparently this brand of yarn was in great demand, as Turner and Company were the only merchants who held any at the time and so were demanding an enhanced price from their Chinese customers. One of the latter demurred, saying he could get the very same material at a lower price in one of the Chinese shops in Endicott's Bazaar. The salesman said this was impossible as Turner and Company held all there was in Hong-Kong. However, the argument ended in the customer producing some, and on inquiries being made, it was found that the missing bale had found its way into the said bazaar, but when or how no man knew.

As the ship was to be mulcted in something like a hundred pounds on account of the short delivery, all inquiries were made on board, and the boatswain, who had been gangway man, remembered seeing the Chinese clerk looking furtively at the mate while he was engaged in erasing some entry from his book. . . . What was thought to have happened was that the mate had called the number, and was about to enter it, when his attention was called off and he had then forgotten it. The Chinese clerk had entered the bale in his book, but on seeing the mate had not done so, erased it. There was no doubt but that the bale had been landed, but Turner and Company never got the yarn. How it ended I cannot say, as we left the harbour soon after.

Another and even more flagrant case was in the following year, when I was third mate in the same ship, but with a different chief. In this case a clerk was taking delivery of cases of confectionery. The bulk of the consignment had been delivered previously, leaving seven to finish. These I had collected and placed by themselves in the 'tween decks, and so informed the mate. When delivering, knowing they were all right, the latter had perhaps taken little trouble in tallying. When Ah-sin was asked to sign the receipt, he blandly requested " one mo' " (another one). Of course Mr. Jeffreys insisted seven were delivered. " No, only six," smiled the clerk, " suppose you no b'leeve my, you come lighter and look see."

I was then appealed to, and, of course, confirmed the mate. We examined the hold of the lighter, and certainly could only see six packages. The mate was in a dilemma—our holds were clear and the missing case was not to be seen in the lighter. It was growing dark, the case was valuable and the mate was in a hurry.

" Get a lamp, one of you," said he, " and we'll turn the condemned junk inside out."

We did so, and searched the lighter from end to end in spite of many obstacles put in our way by the crew of the craft. At last, right aft, in a cunning kind of well in the timbers, covered over with rags of matting, we dragged the missing case to light.

The ship was nearly ready for sea and the mate was anxious to avoid any bother with the police, so he took the law into his own hands. The clerk had to come on board our ship to sign the receipt, when he was promptly anchored by his pigtail, and the enraged mate, with the tail end of a main topgallant clewline, read him a severe lesson on the sinfulness of infringing the eighth commandment.

CHAPTER XVII

FACTORS IN PASSAGE MAKING

SPEED was everything in the tea-clippers, and the factors which made for fast passages were in consequence of prime importance. Superiority of model and equipment were, without doubt, the two most essential points. Yet it was only rarely that a clipper was produced of undeniably better sailing qualities than her rivals, so that this factor was not so prominent as it would otherwise have been.

Eliminating the factor of fortune, good or bad, which would upset all calculations, let us glance at the other and more ponderable forces which made for fast passages.

In the first place came the question of equipment. There would not be much difference in quality between the gear of any two cracks of the tea fleet, but so keenly were they handled that the difference between the unworn canvas of a new ship and that of one on her second or third voyage would be a matter of consequence.

The trim, again, was by no means a negligible factor. Here the advantage would be in favour of the ship not on her first voyage, for in such cases the captain and officers would have better knowledge of the precise trim which suited the ship and be able to act in accordance.

To trim a ship to get the last fathom of speed out of her was not such an easy matter as might be imagined. It was a difficult thing to estimate in a new ship, and had to be judged by her model or by comparison with other vessels similarly constructed. Most clippers would sail better by the wind when on an even keel, but when running free were considered to do better when trimmed a bit by the stern. The Chinese stevedores were past masters in the art of judging trim by the eye. Experience was the best teacher.

Captain Keay of the *Ariel* paid great attention to the trim of that clipper when tea-laden. He was very particular to have her just the right number of inches by the stern. The peculiar construction of the *Ariel* allowed a method to be adopted by which the trim could be varied an inch or two as circumstances required. She was a flush-decked ship, with a clear run of deck from near the knightheads to the taffrail. A strong wooden case, fitted with wheels, was provided and filled with odds and ends of stream chain, etc. This could be dragged right forward when the ship was sailing by the wind, and dragged aft again when running free. During the keen racing days, say until about 1870, this was always in use, but thereafter, the trouble, wear and tear of deck and problematical nature of the advantage gained, caused the contrivance to be done away with.

A third factor was the state of the ship's copper sheathing. This was usually renewed every two years. It was considered that a ship was more speedy during the first year, as when the copper was worn thin by friction it was more easily displaced. It was no uncommon thing to find, after two years' wear, that twenty or thirty sheets of the metal had been torn and wrinkled up in such a manner as to obstruct the vessel's easy passage through the water and so diminish her powers of sailing.

To a certain extent, these were all minor matters in actual practice, yet taken together they had a material influence on the success of a voyage, when the fact of docking three or four hours before a rival might mean the gain of anything from £1,000 to £1,500.

Another point not to be overlooked was connected with the owner of the ship. The one who provided his ship with new equipment gave his captain a great advantage over others whose owners had strict leanings towards economy. To my mind a new suit of sails would make a ship sail a knot faster in light winds than one with a well-worn suit. The latter allowed the wind to blow through them to a certain extent.

Of course, among the half-dozen clippers of recognized powers that would be likely to be in the running from Foochow with the first batch of new teas, every attention would be given to this point. Even if one did not gain the coveted premium, which could only fall to the lot of one, it was still necessary to be close behind the winner to ensure being " laid on the berth " the following season, and so command the highest rate of freights.

Even here luck played sad tricks. I have a recollection of one season (1872, I think) when the cracks were sent away at a rate of, say, £5 per ton. Then something happened which caused a demand for shipping, and the second-rate clippers filled up easily at £6 10s. per ton. This, of course, was a " fluke." Usually the rate dropped about £1 a ton after the first flight of clippers had been despatched.

But I should be inclined to attribute the prime factor in making fast passages to the personal element —the captain and officers of a ship, to wit. Always bearing in mind the proviso that the best commander and most energetic officers who ever sailed the seas could not control Fortune.

Energy, skill and sound nerves, enabling one to carry on longer than a nervous man dared to do, were of the greatest importance in making fast passages. Yet hard driving had its limitations, and he who carried on recklessly defeated his own object. In this connection I might quote the advice given by Captain John Robertson to the newly-appointed chief mate of the clipper *Black Prince* in 1863.

Captain Robertson was the most experienced and successful of the tea captains of early days. Killick, Enright, Maxton and my own father were all considered first-class tea-clipper captains, but none of them were deemed quite the equal of John Robertson. He had been in command of three of the most famous clippers over a period extending from 1844 to 1855. His early fame was gained in *John o' Gaunt,* a great favourite of British tea merchants in Canton before the repeal of the Navigation Laws in 1849, when British shipowners had been discouraged from constructing vessels of an extreme clipper type, owing to the manner in which ships were measured for tonnage.

(A vessel of great length of keel in proportion to beam and depth of hold would be registered as of considerably more tonnage in comparison with her carrying capacity than a short " dumpy " ship with a deep hold and a broad beam.)

The repeal of these laws enabled the *Stornoway* to materialize in 1851, and the experience Robertson gained in her, a vessel of about six hundred and fifty tons, produced the *Cairngorm,* to which he was transferred.

Along with the Thames-built *Challenger,* this vessel made a brave show against the Yankee clippers, whose owners had no obsolete navigation laws to contend with. So much so, that by 1857 the latter were practically ousted from the London tea-carrying trade, which they had dominated since 1849.

In 1863 John Robertson, then a shipbroker in London, became financially interested in the new tea-clipper *Black Prince*, launched that year from the yard of Alexander Hall & Sons of Aberdeen.

The *Black Prince* was designed to be superior to any clipper then afloat, and to achieve that end no effort was left undone nor expense spared. Up to that time the *Fiery Cross* had proved herself the fastest all-round ship in the China trade, although the Clyde-built *Falcon* ran her pretty close. Mr. Rennie of London, who had designed the *Fiery Cross* and given her certain modifications of model which had produced the best results, was engaged to design the *Black Prince,* and it was confidently expected she would be an improvement on her predecessor. Robertson himself saw to her equipment and gave the parting instructions to her officers. Coming from a man of such experience they should go a long way to discount the boastful methods attributed to Blackball skippers, of the " carrying-on-till-all's-blue " school, of whom we hear that they were in the habit of padlocking their topsail sheets when they went below, apparently forgetting that, like " love," a sharp knife " laughs at locksmiths."

" Now, Mr. Henderson," said Captain Robertson to the mate, " there are great things expected of the *Black Prince,* and we trust you will do all in your power to get her along. I have no doubt you have heard the various tales concerning clipper-driving, such as locking topsail halyards and other freaks of that nature, but don't believe them. There is nothing gained in the long run by carrying away spars and splitting sails; what is required is constant vigilance.

Carry on sail as long as possible without risk, but try and get it in in time. And then take the first opportunity of clapping it on again.

"Remember, too, that in light weather the officer of the watch is apt to be absorbed in making the ship look smart for entering port; or perhaps anxious to show a greenhorn how to make a long splice; then, when he happens to look aloft, he finds the weather leaches of the sails lifting.

"Avoid this: leave all such matters to the boatswain. Let it be your constant care to watch the steering; to trim your sails to every flaw of wind; to have every stitch of canvas set that will draw; and to be careful that none of your sails, especially the lee stunsails, are being flogged by others and so pulling aback. Attend to these things and let all other matters give place to them."

Thus John Robertson. If not such spectacular advice, it was a good deal better for making records than the "go at it blindly and break things" recommendation, attributed—wrongfully, I have no doubt—to men who knew better than to act on such advice.

Thus it will be seen that in the case of the *Black Prince*, in order to produce a record-breaking tea-clipper:

> "All was done that man can do,
> And all was done in vain,"

simply because the wrong man was chosen as skipper.

He was a man of bold appearance, not a little given to blowing his own trumpet (which, indeed, was said to have influenced the choice), yet withal a good-hearted gentleman. His name was Willie Inglis. But we may leave the consideration of his seamanship to a further chapter.

CHAPTER XVIII

HOW IT WAS NOT DONE

THE clipper from which such great things were expected was fitted out and Willie Inglis was appointed captain of her. The result serves to bear out my contention that one of the greatest, if not the greatest, factor in making fast passages was represented by the commander.

Inglis had one glaring fault which may have been partially caused by a lack of nerve, or, as I rather think, by a lack of energy. This was his inconstancy of purpose. He would set out boldly to take a certain course, then suddenly and without any apparent reason, change his mind and adopt another. Thereafter, as likely as not, he would revert to his original plan.

For instance, on the second voyage of the *Black Prince*, Henderson still being chief mate, the ship brought a cargo of rice from Rangoon to Hong-Kong. It was the period of the north-east monsoon in the China Sea, and, after clearing the Straits of Singapore, Inglis elected to go north by way of the Palawan Passage, on the eastern side of the China Sea.

He set out to do so, then changed his mind and started to beat up by the Paracels. The ship had reached nearly as far north as Pulo Sapata when stormy weather was encountered, and Inglis funked it. He again determined for the " Palawan."

To adopt this course he had to run to the south-west. He did so for thirty-six hours, then without warning changed his mind again, went about, and came by the middle of the sea after all.

The aggrieved Henderson, who was himself a keen enough sailor and a thorough sail-carrier, reckoned that at least a week was lost by these indecisions. " What encouragement," he wanted to know, " had officers to catch every flaw of wind "—saving at the most a mile or two daily—" when the captain deliberately threw away a whole week? "

The same sort of thing happened on a smaller scale when I made a voyage as an apprentice in the *Black Prince* in 1867. We were proceeding by the eastern route to Hong-Kong. As a rule, after threading the Straits of Timor, the Ombai Passage, Straits of Menapi and so on, ships entered the Pacific by way of the Straits of Gilolo. Captain Innes of the *Serica* had gained something over rivals by entering the Pacific through Dampier Straits, a somewhat narrow yet perfectly safe passage, free from hidden dangers, adjacent to the north-west point of New Guinea. He had advised Inglis to try the same route.

On a fine clear afternoon we approached Dampier Straits in company with a couple of coal-laden north-country barques. Just as we were entering the narrows the wind turned against us. The channel, however, was some eight or ten miles across and, the weather being clear, with prospect of a fine, moonlit night, there would have been little difficulty in working our passage through. The distance to be traversed to get clear of the narrows was only a few miles, and short tacks of an hour, or, as the wind was light, perhaps two, would have sufficed to get us through.

Had the weather been thick or squally the case would have been different. As it was, there was no risk and little difficulty. We had a demonstration of its

M

practicability on the part of the two barques which, blunt-ended as they were, carried on steadily into the Straits. Yet, with such an object lesson, in a ship that was the last word in naval architecture, Inglis's nerve failed him.

Late in the afternoon the watch were ordered to stand by the braces, and Inglis called me aft. I was stationed by the wheel, near the place where the captain was walking excitedly to and fro, looking earnestly at the land and muttering to himself at every turn. As he came to a stand near me I heard him say: "Damnation! what made me take this passage?" The remark was the more surprising, as Inglis very seldom swore.

The mate, who was a man of a very different stamp, perhaps suspecting what was in the captain's mind, deliberately kept out of his way and busied himself forward. Perhaps the matter had been discussed between them previously. At all events, with a stamp of his foot, Inglis suddenly turned to the helmsman: "Put your helm up," said he, and ordered me to ask the mate to square the after yards, and, to the amazement of all hands, the *Black Prince's* head was turned towards the open water.

We ran back for about half an hour till we were well clear of the narrows, then the ship was brought to the wind with the main topsail aback.

We lay thus all night, and a lovely night it was. Towards midnight we had the mortification of seeing the two barques (neither of which could lay claim to being a clipper) sailing past us as they worked to windward. By daylight they were well through the narrows, while we had gratuitously thrown away a full twelve hours.

Of course, as a lad I had no means of knowing on how many other occasions distance was lost. But I often noticed the officers shrug their shoulders and smile at manœuvres, the result of which was not so palpable to the crowd forward as the scuttling out of Dampier Straits had been.

Still, in 1869, we had another instance of Captain Inglis's peculiar brand of seamanship which set all hands swearing, boys and all.

On this occasion we had come via the Gilolo Straits, where we had been in company with a medium tea-clipper, the (second) *Guinevere*. She was bound to Hong-Kong as we were. In no shape or form was she a match for the *Black Prince*.

Our route from the Pacific into the China Sea was by way of the Bashee Channel. The Bashees are a group of half a dozen volcanic islands, lying in a line from north to south, with deep water channels, six or seven miles in breadth, separating one from another. The main channel, however, and the one usually taken, is of considerably less width than this.

We arrived near these islands on the evening of March 7th, with the north-east monsoon blowing and the weather somewhat thick and hazy. Sail was then shortened, so as not to approach the islands before daybreak, and eventually Inglis laid the main topsail to the mast. No doubt this was a justifiable precaution, but we expected to steer for the channel when day broke.

This was not to be. The ship was kept hovering off and on, in the hope that land would appear in sight. For two whole days and nights we held thus, waiting for the weather to clear in order that land could be seen as soon as it rose above the horizon.

Now these islands are hilly and rise steeply from the water, being visible long distances in fine weather. Though ships usually steer for the main channel, there would be nothing to hinder them taking any of the four or five passages through the group, as there are no hidden dangers and the islands can be safely approached within half a mile, perhaps less.

The weather was not so thick but that we could have discerned a ship under sail, or islands like the Bashees, at a distance of four or five miles. There was nothing to prevent a navigator reasonably sure of his latitude from running in until he saw an island, when he would have ample time to alter course north or south as occasion demanded. He could be certain of deep water thereabouts.

But apparently it was too much of an ordeal for Inglis. So we lay dodging off and on till the weather cleared, and wasted two whole days and a bit over in consequence. When we arrived in Hong-Kong we found the *Guinevere* discharging cargo, and she was painfully the slower ship.

Inglis's failing was not unknown, and mates of exceptional ability were provided him, to see if something could not be got out of the *Black Prince* in spite of the peculiarities of her commander. It was all one. Sooner or later the zeal of the best among them came up against the more cautious methods of the master and had to be abated. In spite of themselves they gradually gave way to *laisser faire,* which I have heard translated as : " Let things go to the devil; if the skipper doesn't care, why should I worry ? "

So the following, which I had from Henderson himself, is an indication of how Captain Robertson's sound advice worked out in practice.

Henderson said the wind being fair and the weather propitious, he was hanging on to the main topgallant sail, all ready to take it in the moment it became necessary. Appearing on deck, Inglis glanced aloft and hinted that the sail had better be furled. Henderson pointed out to him that he was ready to do so at a moment's notice if necessary and, apparently satisfied, the captain went below.

Now, in a case like this, most tea-clipper masters, had they felt there was any risk or had any doubt about the mate's ability, would have stayed on deck to watch things for themselves, for the sail was undoubtedly helping the ship. Not so Inglis; distance made good always came second to his own physical, or perhaps it was mental, comfort.

He had not been long off the deck when he reappeared and in a peremptory manner approached the mate. " I thought I told you to take that main top-gallant sail in. Now get it done at once ! " Henderson, with as cheerful an " Aye, aye, sir ! " as he could manage, gave the necessary orders.

No more was said that night, but Henderson did not like to remain under the aspersion of having disobeyed orders and returned to the subject next morning at breakfast. He mentioned the instructions he had received from Captain Robertson, but Inglis broke in with : " Look here, *sir*, I am master of this ship and not Captain John Robertson, and when I give an order, I expect it to be obeyed."

He had his moods; at times I have seen him carry sail as long as ever I have seen my father, who had a reputation in that direction, do so. At others, he would keep the ship dodging under low sail all night, rather than watch the ship himself. On the *Lammermuir* this was never done; sail was invariably made again at the first chance; there was no waiting for daylight with father.

Thus the *Black Prince*, which was really a very fast clipper, suffered in reputation until her name became a byeword and a reproach among sailors, but we just had to grin and bear it. The climax had been reached before I joined the ship. She left Foochow about the middle of the dozen clippers that sailed with the first batch of teas, and was the very last to reach Gravesend. She was known for years afterwards as the " whipper-in."

Captain Inglis had his own share of the chaff, but it never appeared to disturb him in the slightest degree. He had a soul above such trifles and retained his pride and position in spite of all. He was a man of commanding appearance and, as was said, " would never have gone to Hades without an excuse." Though the principal owner would dearly have liked to have supplanted him, " Willie " bore down all opposition. He had nerve enough, in this direction, to face a battalion of " landlubbers " and come off triumphant.

At the same time he was much liked and treated his men generously. No man ever refused to sail a second time with Captain Inglis if he was given the chance.

To hear him talk among his friends one would have imagined he was a second Alexander. Though his conversation often provoked a smile, few among his auditors cared to take him up. If they did, he would almost certainly turn the laugh against them.

Good old Inglis! There was many a worse, though he was never in the running for the " blue ribbon," nor anywhere near it. And though he did nothing else, I must thank him, among other favours for this—that he afforded me, when I came to make passages myself, with an excellent example of " how it was not done."

CHAPTER XIX

AND HOW IT WAS

I HAVE already referred to a few shipmasters who were considered the finest seamen amongst the earlier tea-clipper captains, yet who were all before my time. Among those with whom I was personally acquainted, until steam made tea-clipper racing a thing of the past, I should unhesitatingly give pride of place among passage makers to Captain Richard Robinson, familiarly known as " Dick."

In all his activities, whether afloat or ashore, Robinson was a restless, active man, unsparing to himself as to others. No matter what business he had in hand, he did it with his might and did not let the grass grow under his feet.

Nor did he study much the susceptibilities of others. He was not in consequence very popular with his men. Those who considered their own comfort much preferred the easy-going ways of the captain of the *Black Prince*, for all he was dubbed the " whipper-in," to " Carry-on-and-go-ahead " Robinson.

A comical tale at the expense of Dick Robinson went the round of the clippers in Foochow which were waiting for the market to open in 1867. It received a good deal of publicity, much to the disgust of the individual principally concerned, who appeared as the victim of his own " go-ahead " principles.

It happened that two or three captains were strolling

through the crowded native quarter on Pagoda Island. As they threaded their way down one intricate alley, Robinson, in his usual hasty manner, elbowed his companions aside in his eagerness to be first.

Suddenly turning a corner of the lane he received from a veranda overhead the contents of a utensil which might literally be termed a " stink-pot." Fair and square it caught him, ruining his neat suit of " pongee silk."

Poor Dick was in a wretched plight and had to beat a hasty retreat to his ship, unaccompanied. He had no one to blame but himself and the defects of his favourite motto, and had to suffer the joke against himself as best he might. He must have been glad when sailing day came.

No one could ever accuse Captain Dick of losing distance by running to leeward to dodge a squall. " Luff it up and shake it out of her " was his creed. And whether his ship was alone on the wide ocean or in company with other vessels, he strictly followed out the veteran John Robertson's advice " to let everything else go to keeping the sails trimmed." It is to be presumed that he required sleep, but most of that he obtained on deck, especially when coming down the China Sea. And then it was with " one eye open," as the saying goes. But in this he only carried to extremes what was practised by nearly all other tea-clipper commanders.

With all this he was not given to carrying on till his topgallant masts went over the side. No doubt a spar now and then gave way; but I never heard of him losing a topmast. He had the essential knowledge of a sail-carrier that kept him from cracking on to the breaking-point, as well as the energy and will-power to make sail again at the earliest moment possible and prudent.

The only mishap that I ever heard him being

From photo. in possession of Capt. John Henderson.　"BLACK PRINCE."

Facing p. 184

involved in was in December, 1866, when the *Sir Lancelot*, which he had just joined as master, was totally dismasted near Ushant. But this cannot be attributed to over-driving. The ship was under very low canvas during a violent south-westerly gale, with a very heavy sea running, when her bowsprit snapped short off. It was thereby impossible to keep the vessel off the wind, and the forestay being slackened up, the next recoil from an advancing sea brought the foremast down. This was followed by the main mast and the mizen topmast, much on the same principle as a child demolishes a row of ninepins by knocking over the leader. Nothing was left aloft but the mizen lowermast. Yet Dick took such measures, by means of a " sea-anchor " or drag from the weather quarter, that he succeeded in getting the *Sir Lancelot* before the wind—not an easy matter for a ship in that condition and in a great sea.

He got his ship back into Plymouth, and when new masts were sent down from London, refitted her in record time. During the next three voyages he entirely redeemed that beautiful clipper's character. He made the best passage home in 1867 and 1869, and the second best in 1868.

The 1869 passage was a marvellous performance. It constituted and remained the record—eighty-nine days—from Foochow to Gravesend against the monsoon. Doubtless there was some element of luck about it, but even so, Dick Robinson was the man to take advantage of all the luck that offered.

I fancy one great point that contributed to the *Sir Lancelot's* marvellous success was that her captain had the nerve to take short cuts, through groups and reefs of islands like the Paracels, when a shipmaster would have to trust solely to a good look-out and his own judgment. By doing so it would be possible to obtain a week's sail over more cautious commanders, who would lose days in circumnavigating such risky localities. Such vigilance was a great asset in making quick passages, but there were not many shipmasters who cared to put their seamanship to such a test.

Robinson had become master of the *Fiery Cross* in 1861, and though on his first voyage the ship made a somewhat long passage home, she was nevertheless first of the tea fleet and so gained the customary premium.

In 1863 she was again first, and such an easy first, that it might have been said as it was in the case of the celebrated race-horse " Eclipse "—" *Fiery Cross* first; rest nowhere." Robinson made the passage in one hundred and three days or thereabouts; the best run made by any of the seven clippers that left within a week of her was one hundred and twenty-three; while the *Falcon*, considered as fast as the *Fiery Cross* or nearly so, though leaving the same day as the latter, took one hundred and twenty-nine days. I know fortune favoured Robinson on this occasion, for he arrived in the Thames just in time to escape a long spell of easterly winds outside. Yet against that must be set the tireless-ness which brought the *Fiery Cross* along, and so escaped the adverse luck which befell the others.

Thus, if the golden rule which Robinson followed smacked of rashness, the results justified the means.

In 1865 the *Fiery Cross* was again first ship docked, making the third extra premium that Dick Robinson had put into his owners' pockets. It was said that the £1 extra freight on each ton of tea was the amount of the premium, which would mean a sum of about £3,000.

Doubtless Dick had a share in this and when he left the sea in 1872 was a well-to-do man. But like many other mariners he lost his treasure more quickly than he gained it, by listening to the plausible tale of some land-shark on " how to get rich quick."

A friend of mine in Hong-Kong told me that in 1866

he made one of a party invited by Captain Robinson to go a short distance in the *Fiery Cross* as she worked her way through the Lyee-moon Passage on her way to Foochow.

My friend, or rather my father's, knew something of ships and seamen and was loud in his praises of the fine sailing qualities of the *Fiery Cross*. But he was even more surprised at the extraordinary activities of her captain. He was, he said, like a man on springs : here, there, and everywhere; getting the work of making and trimming sail accomplished in half the time an ordinary skipper would have done. He paid scant regard to appearances : my informant said he had never seen such a " mess "—ropes and gear thrown down and left about the decks anyhow until the operation was complete.

From 1864 to 1869 Dick Robinson's principal rival in the art of carrying sail was Captain Innes of the *Serica*, and later of the *Spindrift*. After the 1866 race it was said that Innes had so exhausted himself in carrying tea he could not even lift a cup of it to his lips without spilling it. Others hinted that tea was not Innes's usual beverage, but I think they were unfair. I believe Innes did occasionally use stimulants when racing, but never to excess. But a little story told of him makes me wonder.

Nutsford, afterwards master of the *Taitsing*, who was mate with Innes in the *Serica*, said that one night, crossing the region of the south-east trades, with the ship under a great press of sail and lying well over to a small gale, he went to call the captain, deeming it would be prudent to take in some of the lesser sails.

Innes, as was customary with him, was reclining on the after lockers below, taking a little rest. When he understood the nature of his mate's inquiry he replied, like the Scotsman he was, by asking another.

" Can ye see the lee cathead still ? " said he, sitting

up. Nutsford gave his commander to understand it was still visible if looked for; whereupon Innes sank back into slumber. " She's a' right then," said he. Nutsford returned on deck and the ship carried on.

Innes may have been pulling his chief officer's leg, for clippers, even if they could stand it, were not constructed to sail on their broadside, yet nevertheless he was a cool customer.

The story prompts me to lay emphasis on another vital factor in successful tea-racing, and that was the experience in the art possessed by the master. A tyro was rarely a match for a veteran.

The shipmaster who had navigated the China Sea for a score of years would be more expert in taking short cuts than a beginner, besides being master of a hundred and one little wrinkles the other could know nothing of. At the same time, increase of experience meant increase of years, and these in turn brought caution. Sometimes, it is true, ignorance was bliss, and a beginner would successfully take risks that a man of more experience would have shuddered at. But on the whole the balance of success was on the side of the veteran.

I might illustrate this by my first voyage in command, when, as a very young shipmaster, I was beaten on the last lap of a well-fought struggle by a man of much greater experience than myself.

CHAPTER XX

IN COMMAND OF A TEA-CLIPPER

In the *Norman Court* after a somewhat tedious passage from the Equator we sighted the island of Terceira on November 19th, 1873. We were bound for London with tea, having left Foochow a day or two before the clipper *Argonaut,* and there was keen competition as to which ship should be docked first.

We had seen nothing of our rival so far, though in the baffling weather we had experienced after losing the north-east trades, it was possible that Nicholson, her master, a noted driver who had been twenty years in the China trade, might be ahead of us.

After passing Terceira the wind came out southerly and we made good way towards the English Channel. I was carrying on " all top-ropes," as the old sea saying goes, to take the fullest advantage of it. Following the example of most tea-clipper captains, I made it a rule to take a nap on the after lockers for an hour or two after lunch, so that I might be able to be on deck at night.

On the 21st we had been sailing with the wind before the starboard beam all the forenoon, having as much wind as we could well swing our royals to. The breeze still increasing, about dinner-time we furled the light sails, and a little later took in the main royal. When I left the deck the ship was staggering along under her three topgallant sails. There was quite

189

enough wind for them, but as it looked like a steady blow and the mate was a careful man, I decided to have my afternoon's rest.

There were no ships then in sight, but when I returned to the deck an hour and a half later the mate pointed out a large ship with fore and main topgallant sails fast, a little abaft our lee beam. He said we had overhauled her out of the haze during the afternoon.

She was not a great distance off, but too far to be sure of her identity. As it was blowing freshly and the weather was none too clear we did not feel inclined to bother with the flag signals. The ship was keeping good time with us, though the mate averred we had come up with her pretty fast. She was sailing under whole topsails and courses when first seen, but, spotting us, had set the main topgallant sail.

The wind was still increasing and the mate was considering taking in our fore and mizen topgallant sails when the stranger shook out her main. That was just as I came on deck. " I fancy," said the mate to me, "that fellow knows us. Isn't that the ship which lay astern of us in Pagoda Anchorage? "

I had a long look at her through the glass and, though she had all the attributes of the *Argonaut*, I could not be sure. I could make out that she carried a full poop and a topgallant forecastle, but these were common adjuncts to all large British ships and were not conclusive. Besides, Sandy Nicholson, her commander, being noted as a sail-carrier, I hardly thought it likely he would have less sail set on the larger *Argonaut* than we on the more tender *Norman Court*.

The haze increasing as the night began to draw in, we soon lost sight of the craft. The two ships had been steering slightly different courses, and when morning dawned there was no sight of her. I came to the conclusion she was not the *Argonaut*. It was her height out of the water which finally decided me; though had I known that she had been aground in the Formosa Channel for twenty-four hours, and that her crew had jettisoned about three hundred tons of tea to get her afloat again, I might have come to a different conclusion.

We had a favourable run to the Channel, encountering some particularly hard north-westerly squalls, with rain and a high sea. In one of them we believed that a brigantine which we passed had come to grief. She was a mile or two astern of us, running under a small topsail, when the squall enveloped her. When it cleared away she was no longer visible. We were running off at some fourteen knots during the squall, and if she had taken in her topsail or it had blown away it is quite possible we might not have been able to see her. Yet many of our people deemed she had foundered. In any case it was impossible for us to attempt to find out. Had we shortened sail and brought our ship to the wind we should have been at least ten miles to leeward of her, with not the slightest chance of being able to reach her, even if anyone had been left afloat.

The weather became still thicker and the sky more overcast. We had been unable to obtain chronometer sights to determine our longitude, though I was sure of our latitude within a few miles. The wind was then westerly and, I thought, ready to back into the southern quarter. Being a young man, with a certificate to lose, I determined to play for safety, and so steered to make a mid-Channel course.

However, by the morning of the 27th, the wind had veered north-westerly, and by that time I judged that by dead reckoning we were athwart the Lizard, galloping up Channel at twelve or fourteen knots an hour.

The weather being still cloudy and no apparent

chance of getting an observation, I thought it scarcely prudent to go capering up Channel without making sure of my position. I was not anxious to lay the ribs and trucks of the *Norman Court* on the French coast, as had been the fate of the fine Australian wool-clipper *Yatala* the previous year.

So orders were given to trim the yards and haul the ship up for the English land, to get a sight of something before night. Of course, we had to shorten sail, which reduced our speed considerably and brought our broadside on to the high seas running up Channel.

I was still keeping as much sail as possible on the ship, which was travelling some eight knots on a north-north-easterly course. The high beam sea made the *Norman Court* appear to be scooping the Western Ocean over her rail in wagon loads. This went on till after dinner. It seemed a pity to be losing distance thus, when we might have been romping up Channel full speed, but, not knowing whether we were east or west of Start Point and this being my first essay at bringing a ship up Channel in half a gale I determined not to risk disaster this time, whatever I might do a second.

However, I was not kept in suspense long. Shortly after dinner—no afternoon nap that day!—I heard the welcome cry of " Land-ho ! " from the look-out man on the fore topsail yard. . . . " Where away ? " . . . " About two points on the weather bow." . . . Sure enough, I made out a lump of land, reaching all round ahead, which soon proved to be the Start. The order was at once given to the helmsman : " Put your helm up : keep her east by south," and to the mate : " Loose the topgallant sails and get a pull on the port braces." And very soon the *Norman Court* was galloping up Channel under all the sail she could carry.

Thus we snored along all night, making sail as

the gale lulled towards morning; and some of the lumbering, timber-laden Quebec-men, jogging along with nothing set above their topsails, must have thought the "Flying Dutchman" was amongst them, as we ran past swinging our main royal.

About 10 a.m. next morning we rounded-to for the pilot off Dungeness. He was some time coming, as there were several other craft in sight to the eastward, hove to, waiting to be served. Meanwhile the *Sir Robert Bruce*, the finest tug on the Thames, spotting a China clipper, had ranged up under our lee quarter, and her master was endeavouring to squeeze an exorbitant price out of me for towing to the dock.

He wanted £80 and was loud in his assurances he would get twice that out of one of the 1,500-ton Quebec ships, which he was hourly expecting.

As a young master I was in a quandary. I knew that the late skipper had never paid more than £50, but I also knew there were a lot of ships coming up, as we had passed through a crowd during the night. They would soon be in sight; and if I did not come to terms with the *Bruce,* as her master took pains to inform me, I might have to follow the example of the *Undine,* one of our rivals from China, which, refusing to pay the sum demanded, had been detained two or three days in the Downs.

The tugmaster also added that neither the *Forward ho*, which had left Foochow ten days before us, nor, so far as he knew, the *Argonaut*, had yet arrived— information which made me all the more eager to secure a tug and get into dock.

So I sprung my offer to £65 and pointed out that he could tow us to dock by next morning's tide, and then have plenty of time to get back to the Ness to get hold of one of the great Quebec-men.

Then the pilot boarded us and took charge and, as

N

he did so, the *Bruce* made a feint of steaming away.
We also filled away, whereupon the tugmaster changed
his mind and shouted that he would accept the offer.
As we had a good fair wind, he said he would not
take our rope till we were round the North Foreland
and had the westerly wind in our teeth.

This was cheering news; and made me more than
ever anxious to dock on the early morning tide. It
was the bait with which the astute tugmaster had got
an extra " tenner " out of our owners' pockets; yet,
as the pilot assured me, if we got the *Bruce* she would
tow us up to Gravesend in time to dock, though it
" blew marlinespikes."

Then another difficulty presented itself. When we
squared away the pilot showed no anxiety to set sail
and, to my disappointment, said there was no need
to hurry, as it looked as if we should have a stiff
westerly wind through the night and, being the
" spratting " season, there would be risk in negotiating the Prince's Channel, and declared his intention
of anchoring in the Downs for the night.

This was a damper. As a youth of twenty-four I
could hardly pit my experience against that of a
Trinity House pilot, so I fell back on diplomacy and
got him to agree to make all haste into the Downs
and not decide as to the rest of the journey till we
reached there.

Then I broached a subject which I thought might
prove interesting and led him into a discussion as to
the water the ship was drawing, from which the
pilotage dues were deduced. He had glanced, of
course, at the figures on our sternpost when he boarded
us, making his calculation that our ship drew nineteen
feet aft. This I disputed, giving him our draft from
the logbook when leaving Foochow, and after pointing
out the urgency of reaching Blackwall by the morning

tide, agreed to sign his note for the full nineteen feet if we managed it.

He saw the point and came to the conclusion the weather might be better than he expected. He promised "to see"; and when we passed Deal, agreed, though with some misgivings, to carry on—"spratters or no spratters."

The *Sir Robert Bruce* all the while had been steaming along close under the land. At one time we thought she had given us the slip. As we swung through the Gull and opened out the North Foreland, she was not to be seen. It was near time to be hauling up for the Prince's Channel and the pilot began to show anxiety and to hint it would be wiser to slip into Margate Roads and make sure of a good anchorage before night.

It was in the nick of time that the *Bruce* made her reappearance and, in response to our signal, came under the lee bow and prepared to take our tow rope, all ready ranged on deck.

Though the wind was now before the beam the *Norman Court* was still snoring along at about nine knots. It was growing dark, and in the narrow waters the task of getting the rope aboard promised to be a lively one.

We hauled the mainsail up, lowered the upper topsails on the caps, and I advised the pilot to haul up the foresail as well, but, not being acquainted with the sailing powers of the ship, he demurred, saying he wanted to keep her under easy command. Then he went forward, leaving me on the poop to look after the steering.

The *Bruce* ranged under our lee bow and hove a line on board to bend on to the clinch of the tow rope. She had to steam pretty fast to keep pace with us and the rope fell short. The tug manœuvred a bit nearer and made a second effort. That too failed and, getting under our bows, she had to go full speed ahead to avoid being run over.

I was getting anxious, as I knew it meant us having to haul up to the westward to get into the Prince's Channel, or having to run away off into the North Sea.

There was a longer interval before the third attempt was made. The pilot made no move. It was not for me to interfere, but the tugmaster, who had done some vigorous shouting when he thought the ship was about to run over him, was not so diffident. As he ranged alongside our starboard quarter, going full speed to keep up with us, a stentorian roar came across the dark waters :

" Haul up that sanguinary great foresail, will ye? How the Hades d'ye think I can get the rope aboard with the ship going through the water like a condemned race-horse? "

That woke the pilot up, and he ordered the hands to get the foresail in. I took it upon myself to luff up until the leaches of the lower topsails were lifting and the ship's way was deadened, while the skipper of the tug made irate remarks as he got the bend of our rope over his towing-hook.

Thereafter he plucked us into the wind and towed us along in great style. We clewed up the topsails, sent all hands aloft to furl them, and settled down for the tow towards London. The wind was now howling through the spars and rigging, but the water kept comparatively smooth and the *Bruce* never looked back, but kept us going at a steady seven or eight knots.

In mariners' parlance, we were " carrying the flood up with us," and with the pilot in charge I was able to get a couple of hours' sleep—welcome enough, as I had spent the previous night dodging outward bounders reaching across Channel under low sail.

By kind permission of Basil Lubbock, Esq.

"SIR LANCELOT."

Facing p. 196

About four bells in the middle watch I was called as the ship was entering the Lower Hope, and we should have to swing before getting into Gravesend Reach so as to drift up past the town to allow the Customs to board us, as well as the mud-pilot. We had no occasion to make fast to a buoy, as we were just in time to reach London with the flood.

We drifted slowly through the Reach, and the new pilot having boarded us and taken over charge, our friend of Dungeness made ready to step into his boat alongside. His "order" was signed to his satisfaction; he had a good stiff nobbler of cognac under his belt, and as many Manila cheroots, with a plug or two of the best Virginia, as he could conveniently carry in his coat pocket. All things considered, he was well fitted to soothe his ruffled feelings as he travelled back to Dover by the early morning train.

I myself was well satisfied and congratulated myself that we had done the best of the four clippers which lay in Foochow with us. Alas! I was to have a rude awakening.

A licensed waterman always joined the ship at Gravesend to assist the pilot and take charge of the wheel as the ship towed up the river. Our regular waterman, whom I had known since I was a child, was one Bill White.

Bill came on board and took his station at the wheel. As we drifted up I noticed a lofty, rakish-looking ship, with a black hull, moored to one of the buoys. I gazed at her with dawning apprehension, then turned to Bill White, who was regarding me whimsically.

"D'ye know her?" he asked dryly.

"It's not Nicholson and . . . ?" I began.

"Yes, it is," said Bill, "that's the *Argonaut*, and Nicholson's in her."

My disappointment was too deep for words, and I

had to turn away to hide my chagrin. If ever one felt victory within his grasp and saw it change suddenly to defeat, I did.

The *Argonaut* had only arrived an hour or two before us, and had been detained at Gravesend owing to some irregularity in her bill of health. I thought we might have passed her off the Western Islands, and knew we had left her in Foochow, and here she was in the river before us, and my " castle in the air " came to Mother Earth with a crash.

Though defeated, I was scarcely disgraced. Sandy Nicholson had been in command of tea-clippers for fifteen years, and in the China trade for another dozen before that, and was considered one of the most skilful shipmasters afloat. Had he contested a race with the redoubtable Dick Robinson himself, he would have made him look to his laurels.

Weighing the matter up, I realized how it was that Nicholson had got in first. Simply through confidence born of experience. We had apparently been equal when entering the Channel. I had played for safety; he, with the assurance of experience, had boldly made a latitude which, by steering due east, would bring him within sight of the Lizard, or the lights thereon. Then, by steering full speed up Channel, he had passed the Start some six hours ahead of us. As it was, we docked a tide before him, and that, after all, was the main thing.

The Clyde-built *Forward Ho*, which had left Foochow nine days before us, did not arrive in London till four days after; and the *Undine*, the fastest of Pile's Sunderland productions, which had left nineteen days before us, took one hundred and thirty-three days against our one hundred and sixteen. The *Maitland*, considered a very high-class clipper, had taken one hundred and twenty days. Had it not been for Sandy

Nicholson I should have made the best passage from Foochow against the monsoon that season. He and I were the only two to face the rigours of the China Sea; all the others had chosen the more easy-going eastern passage.

And when it became known that we had passed the *Argonaut* off the Western Islands, carrying our three topgallant sails while she had them fast, I got all the credit I wanted.

CHAPTER XXI

SOME CLIPPERS COMPARED

IT is a difficult and somewhat invidious matter to say which was the fastest of the clippers that ever sailed from China with teas. Some excelled in light weather, while others required strong breezes in order to show their paces. Unless one has had personal experience of them, no authoritative judgment can be formed, for it is an almost impossible task to decide on the conflicting evidence to be gathered from others. Most seamen are prejudiced in favour of some particular ship, and seldom will a sailor allow that a rival was the faster of any two clippers.

Then again it is not always safe to judge by apparent results, as I have elsewhere endeavoured to show; the masters being often a deciding factor in making good passages. Besides, even when one clipper has shown a decided advantage over another when sailing in company under similar conditions of wind and weather, such proof is not incontrovertible. The relative condition of trim, sails and sheathing must be taken into account; for, should the same two vessels meet on a future passage, it is quite possible their relative positions might be reversed.

Owing to my father's connection with the *Lammermuir*, I had heard much about the tea-clippers before I went to sea in one myself in 1863. From that date until 1880 I was in continual contact with the captains

and officers who sailed in such vessels; indeed, I think
I may safely say I have been on board every one of
the clippers I mention. During that period I helped
to convey more than a dozen cargoes of the early teas
to London. These advantages tempt me to think I am
justified in expressing an opinion, the more so as of
late years so many pronouncements have been made
upon the subject.

After due consideration I am inclined to name the
famous *Ariel*, built and designed by Steele's of
Greenock in 1865, as holding pride of place. Certainly
she was my beau-ideal of a tea-clipper, though I could
name a dozen others which ran her very close, for
among those of the first rank there was indeed little to
choose. Perhaps her compatriot, the *Titania*, was her
nearest approach in both beauty and speed.

Unfortunately the *Ariel* had the defects of her
qualities, and her good points were obtained at the
expense of more sterling attributes, and in the end
proved the cause of her undoing. She was indeed a
very yacht. To ensure a clean " run " she was so cut
away aft that she had no counter at all, and was, in
consequence, a very dangerous ship to manage when
contending with heavy seas.

Her extraordinary fine " run," which was carried
even above the waterline, though enabling her to slip
away from all competitors in light winds and smooth
water, militated greatly against her in other circumstances. So greatly was this the case, that when only
a moderate sea was running, and it became necessary
to go on another tack, it was considered wiser to
" wear " her round, at a considerable loss of distance,
rather than to go about head to wind in the more
usual manner. The reason for this was, as some of
her people told me, that while " in stays " with a fresh
breeze blowing she would fetch sternway so instantly

and at such a rate that she was apt to scoop the water over her taffrail, and, being flush-decked, would wash the ropes lying upon the deck into confusion, and so prevent the men standing at the braces from getting the yards trimmed.

Again, when " running down the easting," or in the roaring forties of the North Atlantic, where mountainous seas arise during westerly gales, it became hazardous to " run " her; and the *Ariel* would be hove to when most other clippers would be scudding before the gale.

In addition to her lack of " bearings " aft, the *Ariel* was handicapped when running before a vicious following sea by her very low bulwarks—lower than those of any other clipper. Her taffrail was brought nearer to the surface of the sea, thus rendering her more liable to be pooped—the term applied to a ship when a wave broke over her taffrail, a very dangerous thing to happen to a vessel.

To illustrate the handicap of which I speak I will quote what I always thought was a very good description of a tea-clipper scudding before a gale. It is taken from the diary of Mr. Frank Logan, a passenger in the *Norman Court* to Sydney in 1879, the ship being at the time south of Cape Leeuwin.

" *May 25th*, 1879.—A very stormy day, a heavy gale blowing; ship under reefed topsails, rolling and labouring in a mountainous sea. . . . Mr. Doughty and I were watching the sea over the stern-rail for some time. It was a grand sight : the high seas rolling along, following the ship. Their crests would break with a roar just as they got near us. We would be on the point of making a bolt from our vantage place, imagining that nothing could stop them tumbling on board and engulfing the poor little *Norman Court*."

"Norman Court."
Andrew Shewan, Commander.

(She was about equal tonnage with the *Ariel*.)   " But lo and behold! her stern would rise in the air and she would be carried along on the top of the wave, with her bow pointing down into the valley, whilst another huge mountain would again be towering above her. ' By Jove ! ' we would say to one another, ' this one is a terror and will be aboard us for a certainty,' but our brave little ship rode out the gale like a cork, although so deeply laden."

I myself sailed in the *Norman Court* for ten years and saw a good deal of this sort of thing. But that ship, though, generally speaking, of as fine lines as the *Ariel,* had a half-poop aft and a full counter from the waterline to the taffrail, which gave her the necessary lifting power and permitted the following seas to roar themselves harmlessly away under her quarters.

Had the *Ariel* been running before such a gale, her lean counter would have afforded no bearings, and a particularly heavy sea, instead of sliding under, might break over the taffrail, filling the deck with water and possibly smashing the steering-wheel—a result which might easily have been fatal to her.

As a matter of fact, this was considered to have been the very fate which overtook her. She sailed from London on a voyage to Australia in 1872, and was never heard of again. She was supposed to have foundered off the Cape when running before a heavy gale, though personally I am not certain but that she came to her end in the North Atlantic soon after leaving New York. That, however, is immaterial; my point is that her unfortunate crew perished owing to the beautiful clean run that I used to admire so much as she lay at anchor in the Pagoda Anchorage of the River Min at Foochow.

Though I hope to give sufficient reasons for thinking that the *Ariel* was probably the speediest clipper of the whole China fleet, I cannot disguise the fact that the difficulties her people had to contend against in stormy weather and high seas may have outweighed, in the long run, her slight superiority in speed.

Even with a moderate beam sea the *Ariel* shipped a lot of water. Her petty officers, who lived in a deck-house amidships, assured me in 1869 that they had a rough time when keeping watch, especially rounding the Cape and approaching the English Channel. They had to dodge in and out of their quarters to prevent their bunks being flooded. On deck scarcely any shelter was afforded by the yard-high bulwarks, and they had to endure, as best they might, the drenching tops of seas that were flung continuously over all.

Owing to a very heavy southerly gale near Cape Agulhas on July 18th, 1868, they said, I recollect, the situation was truly critical. Knowing that the *Taeping* and other clippers were close on his heels, Captain Keay kept the *Ariel* going through a tearing gale and high-confused sea. To use their own words, " the ship ran away with them." Everything movable was swept from the decks; pigsty and pigs, much to the Irish chief mate's sorrow, went bodily over the lee-rail, and the deckhouse was so damaged that they expected it to follow the pigsty. The longboat, standing in chocks abaft the foremast, was stove in; and the front of the monkey-poop, upon which the wheel was elevated a foot or so above the main deck, was badly smashed, until it became a question whether the wheel itself would survive the gale.

Thus the *Ariel* in a heavy sea. Her peculiar qualities have led to a good deal of misunderstanding about her. She was reputed to have outlived fiercer gales than other ships ever encountered. As a matter of fact, it was rarely the extraordinary violence of the wind that brought her into trouble, but the qualities inherent in the ship herself. She had been designed as a superlative flyer in light weather—other considerations were subordinate to that. In the instance mentioned above, the *Taeping* and other clippers came through the same storm, but without suffering to anything like the same extent as the *Ariel*.

Whenever the *Ariel* met her compatriots at sea, she could outsail them. I never heard anyone boast of having slipped away from her, unless by a temporary fluke of wind. Captain Keay, it is true, once admitted that the *Lahloo* once fore-reached and weathered on the *Ariel* when emerging from the " doldrum " region north of the Equator, but the latter ship had a couple of important points in her favour. She was then on her first voyage, so that her copper would be sound and her suit of sails aloft in the best of condition. The *Ariel* was wearing her " second year " copper, and, having been in commission some three years, her fine weather suit of sails would be more than a little worn, which would make an appreciable difference.

Then, again, the *Lahloo* was some miles to windward of the *Ariel* when first encountered, and it is quite possible she had slightly more favourable conditions of weather. I think this is likely, because the *Taeping*, which was to leeward of the *Ariel* on the same morning, dropped astern and to leeward much more quickly than one would have expected her to do if the wind had been at equal strength over the whole area occupied by the three ships. At all events, this is the only occasion, so far as I am aware, of any clipper claiming to have outsailed (even in that slight degree) the *Ariel*. As it was, the latter arrived in dock six whole days before the *Lahloo*.

In the race of 1866, as is well known, the *Taeping* and *Serica* made equal time with the *Ariel* from the River Min to the Downs, and the first-named ran side by side with her all the way from the Lizard to the Thames, but such a thing never occurred again, though opportunities presented themselves in plenty. Though the two ships competed together on more than one occasion after this, it was invariably the *Ariel* which proved the faster. As for the *Serica*, on the next voyage (1867), in crossing the south-east trades, the *Ariel* came up with her, passed her and sank her out of sight astern in thirty-six hours—thus proving herself about " half a knot " the faster ship.

In 1868, after leaving the River Min on May 28th, the *Ariel* passed the *Sir Lancelot*. They were said to be sister ships, though they were not of similar design. No doubt she passed her famous rival pretty slowly, but the fact remains that she did get ahead some distance. Then Captain Robinson, the ever daring commander of the *Sir Lancelot*, took a short cut inside Turnabout Island, and so again became leading ship. And again the *Ariel* passed her.

According to Captain Keay's expressed opinion, the *Ariel* was the better ship of the two when she fell in with the *Spindrift* in the China Sea, and I never heard the statement contradicted.

Thus, all things considered, I think that one is justified as in claiming the *Ariel*—though the difference between herself and the next two or three might be small—was the fastest of all the China clippers. Her biggest day's work of three hundred and forty miles is equal to the best of the *Thermopylæ's* runs; and the claim of the *Cutty Sark* to a twenty-four-hour run of three hundred and sixty-three miles I believe to be mythical. The fact that the *Taeping* held her own with her in that famous race up Channel in 1866 I hold to

be attributable to the trim of the *Ariel* on that occasion.
It was discovered afterwards that the matter of her trim
made a perceptible difference to her speed. Captain
Keay, as I have already mentioned, contrived a device
by means of which he could trim his ship at sea,
adapting her to cope with a head wind or a fair
one.

I have no record of the *Ariel* meeting either the
Thermopylæ or the *Cutty Sark* at sea. This is a pity,
as owing to their longevity these two vessels are
popularly conceived to have been the fastest ships afloat.
My own belief is that, given moderate weather and
smooth water, the *Ariel* would have been more than a
match for either of them. In heavy weather their
superior beam might have weighted the scales in their
favour; but, even so, I think the *Ariel* would have held
her own with her more powerful rivals—if at a greater
risk.

I myself met the *Ariel* twice at sea. Once, in 1868,
when homeward bound in the *Black Prince*, while we
were running into the chops of the Channel, the *Ariel*
passed close to us, outward bound, and standing south
on the starboard tack. I was but a youngster at the
time, and was up aloft loosing the topgallant sail.   I
had a good view of her, slashing through the water,
her men aloft reefing the fore topsail.   She certainly
looked every inch a clipper—very low in the water,
travelling very fast, and apparently shipping much
water.

Coming home, she had taken the shine out of the
rest of the tea fleet, ourselves included, for she had left
Foochow four days before us, and here she was, well
on her way to China again. The *Fiery Cross* was
equally badly beaten, and the famed *Titania* from
Shanghai, even worse.

On the other occasion on which I remember

encountering the *Ariel*, Captain Keay claimed that he had weathered on our ship, the same *Black Prince*. It was contrary to my recollection, but I was not in such a good position to judge.

We were working south along the Cochin China coast, between Capes Varella and Padaran at the time. The land breeze had subsided and in endeavouring to get an offing we met the *Ariel* standing in from seaward. She had come along outside the Paracels, but getting a south-easterly slant had kept her board on to the Cochin China land, a lucky thing to do. About ten in the morning it fell calm and so continued till 1 p.m., the *Ariel* then being about five miles to seaward of us. Then the sea breeze sprang up, and, before it reached us, we saw the *Ariel's* sails fill and watched her reach away to the south-west. She was hull down before we were able to make a move.

The *Ariel* seemed to be in perfect trim that voyage. She had been newly coppered in China, besides getting a new outfit of sails, a suit having been lost on the coast of Japan, when she was thrown on her beam ends through her cargo of rice shifting. It was on this occasion she passed the *Serica* so quickly, as well as the *Belted Will* and the *Whiteadder*. She finished up the passage by getting to windward of the *Fiery Cross*, in a three days' tussle with that ship against easterly winds at the mouth of the Channel.

By 1866 a few of the tea-clipper owners were beginning to doubt whether they had been doing the right thing in producing ships of the *Ariel* and *Taeping* type, as their lack of beam, though tending to speed in light winds, made them very tender and in need of much ballast under a cargo of tea. For this reason the *Titania*, launched for the same owners as the *Ariel* in 1866, and the *Spindrift*, built for Findlay & Company in 1867, were given a beam of nearly 36 feet, or three

more than that of the *Ariel* and five more than that of
the *Taeping*. They were followed by the *Leander*
(1867), *Thermopylæ* (1868), *Cutty Sark* and *The
Caliph* (1869).

In spite of her greater beam, to outward appearance
the *Titania* was almost as sylph-like as her predecessor.
She was often erroneously spoken of as a sister ship.
But Shaw, Maxton & Company, her owners, had learnt
something from the *Ariel's* first voyage, and the *Titania*
was given 36 feet of beam as against the *Ariel's* 33 feet
9 inches, as well as some three feet more length of keel.
I think, too, she was rather fuller under the counter and,
instead of being flushed-decked, was given a short
monkey-poop, with a house on deck aft for a cabin.
She had also a house forward to accommodate
the seamen and petty officers, which occupied the place
held by the longboat in the *Ariel*.

These advantages, if they slightly militated against
her in light winds, enabled her to keep going with safety
longer than the *Ariel,* and would in the long run cause
her to be more dependable than her ticklish forerunner.
Indeed, her performances bear this out. Though under
her first commander, Robert Deas, an elderly man whose
" driving " days were over, she made comparatively
long passages, matters were altered when men like
Captains Burgoyne and Dowdy took charge of her.
These in turn were relieved by men of mediocre
experience, and again she was compelled to do second
rate work.

The *Ariel's* quickest passage from Foochow to
London was ninety-seven days. Under Captain
Burgoyne the *Titania* came home from the pilotage
grounds at Shanghai in ninety-six days. In 1871
Captain Dowdy actually brought her home from
Foochow (in the strength of the south-west monsoon) in
ninety-three days. On this occasion she was sixty-five

O

days from Anjer, in the Straits of Sunda, to London, which constitutes a record.

These were better passages than were ever made by the *Cutty Sark*, though I attribute the fact largely to the superior skill and experience of their respective captains, rather than the quality of the ships. Captain Wallace stated that the *Cutty Sark* and *Titania* ran neck and neck for some forty-eight hours in strong trade winds between St. Paul's Island and Java Head; and it is also recorded that the *Titania* was the first ship to have sight of the above headland by some twelve hours. From this it would appear that the latter was slightly superior in strong winds, and if such was the case it is not likely that the positions would have been reversed in light winds. We have it on no less authority than that of Captain Selby, who resigned the post of chief mate of the *Cutty Sark* to take command of the *Titania*, that the latter was an equally speedy ship.

The *Spindrift* was a very beautiful ship, very fast with strong winds abeam. She was very heavily sparred, and it was said of her she was " like a giblet pie, all legs and wings." The only two passages she made from Foochow, ninety-seven days in 1868, tying for first place with the *Ariel*, and one hundred and six days in 1869, sailing by the longer eastern passage, prove that she was no sluggard. Being fuller under the quarters and fitted with a half-poop enabled her, in combination with her greater beam, to stand up well against heavy weather.

I never heard of the *Spindrift's* performances in company with any other clipper, yet I was well acquainted with Innes, her captain, and a number of men who sailed in her, and they pronounced her to be " a galloper," that is, very fast when running free. I think it quite possible she was almost equal to the *Ariel* with the yards off the backstays, and perhaps a little better in very strong winds. The *Spindrift* was built, and I think designed, by Connell's of Glasgow.

Another of " the Clyde-built beauties," designed by Mr. Waymouth, an official of Lloyds, London, was the *Leander*. She resembled the *Ariel* more closely than did any other clipper, unless perhaps it was the *Titania*. She was exceedingly sharp both forward and aft, and, like the famous American-built *Flying Cloud*, the fastest of the California flyers, had a very short bilge amidships, the " run " commencing almost where the bow left off. She looked an out and out " heeler," and made a number of fine passages, especially in the New York tea trade from China. Her reputation suffered, however, in consequence of her being passed at sea in a fair struggle with the great *Thermopylæ*. Yet she was to a certain extent handicapped on that occasion, though, as it was owing to a fault in her construction, the honours must still go to the *Thermopylæ*.

The fact was that the *Leander* had such fine lines, that when loaded down to her Plimsoll mark she " lifted " little more than her registered tonnage, while other clippers like the *Sir Lancelot* and the *Thermopylæ* easily lifted a fourth more than that. Now, in 1869, through some error made in shipping the necessary ballast for tea, it was found that the *Leander* could not be fully laden without putting her deeper in the water than her Plimsoll allowed. So some chests of tea were broken out of the stowage and about fifty tons of ballast removed. Even this did not permit her hold to be filled quite full.

As it was, she rode very deep and her marks were out of sight in the fresh water, while the *Thermopylæ* probably had six inches of freeboard.

The *Thermopylæ* left Foochow two days after the *Leander* and passed Anjer on July 28th, only sixteen hours behind. On August 2nd the *Leander* was sighted ahead, but it was not until the 5th of the month that she was dropped out of sight astern. Thus the *Thermopylæ* had gained about twenty-four miles in the three days, during which time she had averaged about nine knots an hour.

Considering that the *Leander* was immersed about a foot deeper in the water, this was not much to boast about, and I think had the two ships been equal in the matter of draft, their sailing powers would have proved about the same. The race from Foochow to this point had been fought out without much advantage gained on either side, but thenceforward the *Thermopylæ* went ahead and eventually reached Gravesend ten days ahead of her rival.

Yet I am sure the *Leander* could sail with the best when her idiosyncrasies as regards trim had been mastered. Captain Knight, who commanded her from 1870 onwards, assured me that she was wonderful when running free in strong winds, and backed up his statements by showing me her logbooks. I remember noting two or three very quick passages of about eighty-five days from Amoy to New York, in which trade she was latterly engaged.

Before going on to speak of the two great rivals, perhaps the best known of all the clippers, the *Thermopylæ* and *Cutty Sark*, I feel impelled to mention the much-talked-of clipper, *The Caliph*.

She was the last production of that world-famous firm of tea-clipper builders, Alexander Hall & Sons, of Aberdeen, and was launched in 1869. Designed on somewhat novel lines by William Hall, her principal features were an unprecedented amount of deadwood amidships, with a sharp rise of floor and a greater beam than usual.

She left London for Shanghai in October, 1869, and

made a fast passage of about one hundred days. From China she sailed to New York, then returned to China, making the passage, I believe, in under ninety days to Anjer. At all events it is said she came up to expectations and a bit over, though I have no authoritative records. However, Captain John Henderson, who had sailed in the *Black Prince, Thermopylæ, Samuel Plimsoll* and *Loch Carron,* and who had acted as captain of *The Caliph* between Aberdeen and London on her maiden trip, often declared that she was the fastest ship he had ever put foot aboard.

Apparently on her passage from New York to China in 1870 she passed through the Straits of Sunda, for she was reported as passing Anjer. But from that day to this nothing further was ever heard of her. What became of ship and crew has never been revealed, and now probably never will " until the sea gives up its dead."

It was not the season of typhoons when she disappeared, and had she been cast away on a reef something would have been heard of her, or some vestige of her would have been left. Had she been burnt in open water some members of her crew would probably have escaped; unless—which seems to me the most likely theory—some explosive had been stowed amongst her general cargo, with the result that both ship and crew were blown to atoms.

Most mariners, however, were of opinion that she had been captured by a fleet of Chinese fishermen pirates, and the ship destroyed after being thoroughly ransacked. This is not improbable, for had *The Caliph* got hard and fast on a reef like the Pratas, where fleets of junks congregate (ostensibly fishermen, but pirates whenever opportunity offered, whose policy in a case of this kind was " dead men tell no tales "), it is quite possible no news of the tragedy would ever reach European ears.

Thus *The Caliph* passed out; an unknown quantity when she floated, and the theme of an unsolved mystery ever since.

CHAPTER XXII

THE " THERMOPYLÆ " AND " CUTTY SARK "

IN 1868 the great *Thermopylæ* was launched from Walter Hood's yard at Aberdeen. Though I think she was not the equal of the *Ariel* in smooth water, she was probably the best all-round ship of the tea-clipper fleet.

Judging from her actual passages, she undoubtedly holds the lead. From the outset she was fortunate in her captains; in the first part of her career exceptionally so. Captain Kemball, though not one of their own men, was chosen by the owners to take command of her when new, over the heads of their own veterans, largely because he had, in the hitherto somewhat lethargic *Yangtsze* beaten much faster ships such as the *Taitsing* and *Black Prince* on her homeward passage in 1867.

It is true that on her most remarkable first voyage, when she broke three records, she was extraordinarily fortunate in the winds she encountered. My uncle was chief mate of her on that voyage, and always admitted that this was the case.

None the less it was an astonishing performance. Her three passages, each of which was a record, were as follows: London to Melbourne, sixty-three days (to Cape Otway, sixty-one days); Newcastle, N.S.W., to Shanghai, from pilot to pilot, twenty-eight days; and ninety-one days *against the monsoon* from Foochow to Gravesend.

Again from Gravesend to Shanghai by way of Melbourne, where she discharged a general cargo, and Newcastle, where she loaded a full cargo of coal, she was only one hundred and twenty-six days. She actually arrived in Shanghai ahead of a ship which had left London before her, bound directly for that port.

Her record passage home, ninety-one days from Foochow to Gravesend, she only held for twelve days. The *Sir Lancelot,* under the invincible Dick Robinson, turned up at Gravesend on October 14th, only eighty-nine days from Foochow. This was undoubtedly the best passage from China, taking the monsoon into consideration, ever made by a sailing-ship.

Both ships had, as the Irishman affirmed, " the luck of a pleeceman " in getting down the China Sea that year. The *Sir Lancelot* was but twenty-one days from Foochow to Anjer, which for many ships would not have been considered a bad passage even in the north-east monsoon. Indeed nearly all the clippers leaving Foochow that season made exceptionally quick passages down the China Sea. My own lucky star was not in the ascendant just then, for this was the only year I came home by the eastern passage and so missed the opportunities afforded the others.

As regards the sailing powers of the *Thermopylæ* when alongside other clippers at sea I had some experience myself, having fallen in with her in February, 1871, while " running the easting down " in the *Norman Court.* Though the conditions were to a certain extent against us, we held our own with the redoubtable White Star ship.

The *Norman Court* at the time was laden as deep as a sand-barge, down to her marks and a little over. We were bound to Shanghai with a cargo of lead, pig and scrap-iron, with chalkflints below; the fine goods consisting chiefly of heavy Manchester bales, a cargo of such weight that the ship's 'tween decks were practically empty.   The *Thermopylæ*, on the other hand, was chockful of the usual lively Melbourne cargo, drapery and hatboxes, with a freeboard of at least six inches. She had, besides, been newly coppered in London, while the yellow metal of the *Norman Court* was in its second year—a quite appreciable disadvantage.

At the time of our encounter we were running east in about 40 south latitude, between the meridians of St. Paul's Island and Cape Leeuwin.   Being bound to Shanghai we were steering for the south-west cape of Tasmania, running dead, at nine or ten knots, before a westerly wind, with everything up to the skysail set on the main and the usual stuns'ls on both sides.   As was customary, we had the mainsail fast, as well as all the after canvas, with the exception of the mizen topsail.

The *Thermopylæ*, which, as we heard later, had been running the easting down a couple of degrees farther south than ourselves, came in sight broad on our starboard quarter about noon.   She was apparently hauling up north for Cape Otway, as she was steering some three points more northerly than we were, having all her sails drawing, with port stuns'ls set only.   Thus she drew across our stern, and as night fell was lost to sight about a couple of points abaft our port beam.   By the bearings taken when first sighted, and again when last seen, we concluded she had made no more easting than we had, and as that was her object at the moment, had gained nothing on us.

As a further proof that there was little difference in the speed of the two ships I would say that on the day, March 2nd, the *Thermopylæ* entered Port Philip Heads, we in the *Norman Court* rounded Cape Pillar, the south-east point of Tasmania.

In point of fact, being bound, as I say, to Shanghai, we reached that port in one hundred and three days from the Lizard, which I think was not far behind the famous performance of the *Thermopylæ* in the previous year.

I have a note of an encounter which the Aberdeen crack had with the beautiful Thames-built tea-clipper *Lothair*, a vessel some two hundred tons smaller than herself. Captain Taylor, one time commander of the Pacific Steam Navigation Company's steamer *Orbita*, who was an apprentice in the *Lothair* at the time, was my informant.

He said that on the occasion in question the *Thermopylæ* undoubtedly proved herself the faster ship, though the conditions prevailing were in favour of the larger vessel. Both ships were sailing by the wind into a stiff head sea, a state of affairs which loaded the dice in favour of the bigger ship.

Nevertheless, all things considered, had I to vote on the subject, I should " plump " for the *Thermopylæ* as the best all-round tea-clipper of her day, inasmuch as she carried a comparatively large cargo of tea over a moderate amount of ballast.

I know that on this point I differ from an eminent modern historian of the clipper-ship era. Mr. Basil Lubbock has called the *Cutty Sark* " the fastest ship that ever left the ways." It is a difficult point to decide; the *Cutty Sark* to-day is a clipper whose name is known all over the world, and I venture to think that it is more from the fact that she is still with us than from any particular performance she made as a tea-clipper, that she owes her reputation as the fastest ship ever built.

When I was second mate of the *Blackadder*, a new iron ship belonging to John Willis, and said to be constructed on much the same lines as the *Cutty Sark* and *Hallowe'en*, that is, after the lines of the *Tweed*, also belonging to Willis, I saw the *Cutty Sark* enter the Blackwall Dock in January, 1870, on her arrival from the Clyde, a brand new ship. She was very much admired at the time and looked every inch a tea-clipper, but, as transpired later, had serious faults of construction (not in her hull, but in her gear), owing to being hastily finished.

Her owner, John Willis the younger, had made cheap contracts for his three new tea-clippers. Messrs. Maudslay, Sons & Field, who were primarily an engineering firm, started a shipbuilding yard at Greenwich, and undertook to build the *Hallowe'en* and *Blackadder* at an unprecedently low rate for the Thames. Both ships were turned out very roughly, insomuch that the *Blackadder* was dismasted six weeks after leaving London; and there was a lawsuit over the acceptance of the *Hallowe'en*.

A shipbuilding firm on the Clyde were given the contract to build the *Cutty Sark*. They became bankrupt before she left the stocks, and the ship was finished off hurriedly by another firm. The consequence was that much of her ironwork was scamped, and on her first voyage Captain Moodie complained bitterly of her weakness in this respect. In her great race with the *Thermopylæ* in 1872, she lost her chance of winning through her rudder collapsing off the Cape—a queer accident which, so far as I know, never happened to any other clipper.

It has been said that John Willis had the *Cutty Sark* designed and built on purpose to lower the records of the Steele clippers, particularly the *Thermopylæ*. If this were indeed so, he never achieved his object. I do not think the *Cutty Sark* ever made a record passage, though her averages in the London-Sydney trade were equal if not better than those of any other ship.

She was undoubtedly exceedingly fast in strong

winds, though I think the record days' runs she was reported to have made will not bear analysis. I have an idea that she dragged a bit in light winds on account of her hollow lines forward. At least it is recorded that the tea-clipper *Wylo*, a vessel of no great pretensions and never considered a flyer, once outsailed her in the light winds of the Java Sea.

These claims were first put forward in a correspondence over the speed of the tea-clippers in the periodical *Fairplay* about the year 1892. There " One Who Knows " wrote: " Permit me to give my quota of evidence to this ship's (i.e. *Cutty Sark's*) extraordinary performances. At an early period of her career she made three hundred and sixty-two and three hundred and sixty-three knots on two consecutive days."

These record runs, it is stated, were made in the " Roaring Forties " of the Southern Ocean. But on looking into them one finds that the ascertained distance was by " dead reckoning "; that by observation was much less.

To account for the difference an adverse current was postulated—a westerly current against hard westerly and north-westerly gales !

What it amounts to is this : they imagined their position was some seventy miles ahead of where it proved to be. Instead of admitting the possibility of error in their reckoning, they assume it to be absolutely correct. The ship had made that distance through the water : hence, as the sun proved they had not done so over the ground, there must have been a current setting them back that distance. The possibility of error in their dead reckoning is ignored; it must be a never-otherwise heard of current that sets down on them on the very occasion they broke all previous records made by clipper-ships.

Now I would ask any man who has navigated a ship about the 44th parallel of south latitude if he ever experienced a strong westerly current there? I am sure the answer would be in the negative. Indeed, with such a current running in the teeth of a fresh west-north-west gale there would be such a confused sea that a hard-driven ship would be almost certain to have her decks swept. Yet the log quoted does not record the *Cutty Sark* even shipped a sea.

The records of currents thereabouts are all the other way. There is a continuous easterly set to the southward of the 40th parallel in the Indian Ocean, as is abundantly proved by bottles cast adrift, and by the logs of ships from East India Company days onwards.

The *Trial*, East Indiaman, was wrecked on the North-West Cape of Australia at a time when her commander considered himself three hundred miles to the westward of that promontory. Another ship, the *Colchester*, bound to Madras, having run her easting down in about the latitude of 40 south, steered north to make the east coast of Ceylon.

High land was descried, but on the starboard bow. The master naturally concluded he had fallen to the westward of Ceylon and hauled his ship on a wind, with the intention of beating south and getting to the eastern side of the island. His astonishment was profound when he discovered it was not Ceylon but Sumatra that he had made.

The *Cutty Sark's* westerly current simply will not stand. Yet the resultant record-breaking claim has often been reiterated and has been capped by another no less unlikely. Under the pseudonym of " Master Mariner " a writer assured the public that the *Cutty Sark* had run a distance of 2,163 miles in six consecutive days, naïvely adding that " she must have travelled 370 miles on one or more days."

tea-clippers was gained in the *Black Prince* and the *Norman Court*.

In the former we could sail on equal terms with the *Serica* and *Taitsing*, and had a little superiority over the *Fiery Cross*. As for the ships I have mentioned prior to these, they were too heavy metal for us.

In the *Norman Court*, a decidedly faster ship than the *Black Prince*, we could keep company off and on with the *Sir Lancelot*. We did so on one occasion all the way down the China Sea. We were very equally matched with the *Kaisow*. We kept time with her from the Lizard to the Cape, sailing in company day after day. She was considered to be a wonderfully fast ship in light winds.

In certain conditions of weather, such as meeting a head sea, the *Norman Court* was slightly superior to both her and the *Sir Lancelot*.

In the spring of 1871, being bound from London to Shanghai, we fell in with the *Sir Lancelot*.

The *Norman Court* had been hung up for a couple of days by a dense fog in the neighbourhood of the Saddle Group of islands. When the fog cleared somewhat we found ourselves not far from a clipper-ship coming along with stunsails set. She proved to be the *Sir Lancelot*, who, it appeared, had not yet experienced any fog. Neither of us were very sure as to our position, and as we made sail to our three royals, the *Sir Lancelot* hauled in her stunsails. She sheered in alongside of us, close enough for the two captains to carry on a conversation.

The *Sir Lancelot* was also from London. She had left twelve days before us and we had gained on her so largely owing to the fact that we had come by a different route. During our conversation the wind was threatening to increase, but the lingering fogbank prevented us from seeing anything of the islands.

For some time, at the rate of nine or ten knots, the two ships ran neck and neck. Then the fog closed down again, and each of us sheered off on opposite tacks. While we were in company we could not detect the slightest difference in our respective speeds, and personally I much regretted we had not the opportunity of noting the result of a twenty-four-hours' trial.

Our second encounter with her was in the Formosa Channel on July 28th, 1874, when both ships were bound to London, we being from Foochow and the *Sir Lancelot* from Shanghai. When first seen, the *Sir Lancelot* was some four or five miles ahead of us. I quote here extracts made in my notebook at the time :

"July 29th, noon: *Sir Lancelot* ahead. . . . July 30th, noon: *Sir Lancelot* abeam. . . . July 31st, noon: *Sir Lancelot* astern."

On the 31st we were encountering the tail end of a typhoon; the weather was bad, and we lost sight of one another.

In justice to the *Sir Lancelot* I should say that throughout these three days we were meeting a rather high south-westerly swell, the result of a storm raging farther south. This was the point of sailing in which the *Norman Court* excelled. Like the *Fiery Cross*, *Black Prince* and other ships designed by Mr. Rennie, the *Norman Court* was especially modelled to cope with head seas. Under such conditions we once sank the *Kiasow* hull down astern in the course of a single day, only to come across her some days later when the weather conditions had changed.

Much the same thing happened on this occasion with the *Sir Lancelot*. Parting company on July 31st, we fell in with her again on August 2nd. Sailing by the wind, with light and moderate breezes, we continued together till the 6th.

P

was the faster ship, and I heard later that her old Aberdonian master was much disgruntled at what had happened. He had no idea that the *Norman Court* could play such tricks with the ship of whose powers he had much cause to boast.

As regards the *Harlaw*, a vessel considered equal to the *Yangtsze* and the *Coulnakyle*, we once passed Anjer some five days behind her. About 9 degrees north of the line in the Atlantic we sighted her and passed her easily in the strong breeze. We overhauled her at the rate of about a knot an hour, but the weather being thick and rainy we soon lost sight of her astern. We met with much easterly winds in the Channel, and eventually arrived at Gravesend five days ahead of her.

There may be one or two other clippers which I have overlooked, whose names are deserving of mention among the select band of the racing fleet. The *Wylo* was one of them, perhaps, though I do not think she was built to contend on equal terms with the racers. She was a pretty vessel and speedy, of course, but she was designed primarily to carry a fair cargo of tea over a comparatively small amount of ballast. One can seldom have it both ways; to gain cargo capacity speed must be sacrificed—partially, at least.

I think I have mentioned the names of all the most famous vessels. There were others, of course, capable of not quite so much as these, which yet endeared themselves to those who sailed in them, so that they remember with advantages some day's run or passage otherwise unrecorded. The fact remains that these were acknowledged indisputably first in their day, and it is not likely the verdict will ever now be reversed.

I mention the fact as I have at different times noticed all sorts of claims in the press. Ships that one never heard of at the time have since been brought forward as the heroes of astonishing performances.

One may take as example the *Flying Spur*. A man who served in her has left on record tales of her prowess that make those who knew the actual ship rub their eyes. He claims that she equalled the 1869 record of the *Thermopylæ* from England to Shanghai, by way of Australia. The " wish " was father to that record : there never was such a performance as that of the *Thermopylæ* on her maiden voyage, either before or since.

The *Flying Spur* is also stated to have passed the *Lightning* easily. One can only credit it if they were on opposite tacks. The *Norman Court's* run of 2,049 miles in a week the writer caps with one of 2,100 miles. Had the *Cutty Sark's* run of 2,163 miles in a week, mythical though I believe it to be, been heard of at the time he wrote, what he would have got out of the *Spur* I shudder to think.

His crowning feat was sailing round the *Maitland*, one of Pile's Sunderland clippers, near St. Helena. It sounds possible enough on paper, but I have been in company with both ships and am prepared to swear the *Flying Spur* never did it—unless the *Maitland* were at anchor. In any other circumstances the Wearside ship would have made short work of such a rival.

But I can hazard a guess as to what prompted this latter yarn. The author continued his practice of making his ship go one better than all the acknowledged record-breakers.

On the passage in question the *Maitland* was actually passed by another clipper in the south-east trades—but it was the *Sir Lancelot*, not the *Flying Spur*, a very different proposition.

The *Maitland* carried a big spread of canvas, and at the time had got every stitch of it set. When the *Sir Lancelot* overhauled her, she had a " dig " at the *Maitland's* expense. She is credited with having hoisted a signal to the effect that " if the *Maitland* could not add something more to her array of moonsails and skysail stunsails, Captain Robinson would be regretfully obliged to leave her."

Other writers, again, would have us believe that the earlier tea-clippers, such as the *Chrysolite, Cairngorm, Challenger, Lord of the Isles, Robin Hood, Friar Tuck, Ellen Rodgers, Kate Carnie*, etc., were equally as fast as the later clippers, but this is not the case. Great improvements were made about that time in ships' models, and this improvement was reflected in the speed of the various ships. Moreover, the accounts of the early passages of these ships were from the reports of those who sailed in them, unconfirmed by documentary evidence, and were only put on paper a number of years after the events in question. When we examine their later passages, as taken from the shipping gazettes, we find the times taken between China and London considerably longer.

To take only one instance. It is recorded that the *Challenger*, on her first eight passages from Shanghai to London, made an average of one hundred and ten days. When we examine the logs of seven of these passages, we get an average of one hundred and fourteen days, a material difference.

The *Robin Hood* was said to have run three hundred and sixty knots in twenty-four hours, and to have averaged three hundred daily for a week. Yet on two occasions she was over one hundred and twenty days (one hundred and thirty-seven in one instance) from Foochow to London. Her best recorded performance was a hundred days from Foochow, sailing in September. Unless there is a mistake in dates, she indeed appears on this occasion to have made a seventy-one-days' run from Anjer. If so, it was very good indeed, although not more than might be expected of a ship that could average fifteen knots for a twenty-four-hour day.

SHEWAN-BARNET. On the 25th January, 1876, at Bow Parish Church by the Rev. G. T. Driffield, Andrew Shewan, Master, Ship "Norman Court" (Tea-Clipper) to Agnes, younger Daughter of Thomas Barnet, Arbroath.

From THE TIMES, *January 27th, 1876.*

We twa hae lingered on the braes
    And pu'd the gowans fine,
And wandered mony a weary fit,
    Since the days o' Auld Lang
        Syne.
                Burns.

But ever with a frolic welcome
    took
The thunder and the sunshine.
                Tennyson.

1926.
" AULD LANG SYNE."
Captain and Mrs. Shewan's Golden Wedding.

Facing p. 239

Captain Enright claims to have run three hundred and twenty-one miles in one day in the little *Chrysolite*, of four hundred and ninety tons. Yet, later in her career, when larger crews were carried and all sorts of flying kites and stunsails provided, she was over one hundred and forty days coming home. We could hardly claim more than that for the *Norman Court*, yet the *Norman Court* only once took one hundred and twenty days from Shanghai, and that was at a time when crews had been cut down and stunsails abolished.

No! the *Stornoway* and *Chrysolite* were probably good twelve-knot ships, while the *Cairngorm*, *Robin Hood* and *Challenger* might work up to thirteen on occasion. But that was all; if they ever reached the fourteen limit (which I doubt), it would be just for a short time, at the height of a gust.

Occasionally we find a ship—though the credit, or blame, may lie with the captain—very consistent in the time she took over certain passages. Thus, the *Black Prince*, under Captain Inglis, made seven passages from Foochow against the monsoon. Her best passage was one hundred and sixteen days, and her longest one hundred and twenty-two, a remarkably uniform performance. On the other hand, the *Titania*, on one occasion ninety-three days from Foochow, just two years later, under a different master, took one hundred and thirty-seven. Yet it is hardly worth while following this up. Fortune, to name no other factors, often took a hand in the game, and we are assured that " the battle is not always to the strong, nor the race to the swift."

In conclusion, one is tempted to say a few words about the extraordinary day's runs recorded in connection with several of the American-built clippers, the *Lightning*, *James Baines*, *Red Jacket* and others of that ilk. It was said that on several occasions runs of four hundred and thirty nautical miles (and even more) were made in the twenty-four hours; and as the said runs were made while steering east in high southern latitudes, the actual time of sailing would be little more than twenty-three hours.

If this were true, a remarkable coincidence at once obtrudes itself on our minds. Though these vessels, mostly units of the famous Blackball Line, were capable of such astonishing performances, although they ran from Liverpool to Melbourne for a dozen years or so, at the height of the gold rush, flying light and full of passengers, yet not one of them ever made a passage comparable to that, say, of the *Thermopylæ* on her first voyage. The *Thermopylæ* once made a run of three hundred and forty miles in the twenty-four hours; these ships were (apparently) capable of sailing round her; yet, when actual passages are compared, not one of them can hold a candle to the White Star crack. How is it?

If the Yankee clippers were capable of such speeds, they should have made the run in about forty-nine days, as against the *Thermopylæ's* sixty. In actual fact, the quickest passages made were those by the *James Baines*, *Lightning* and *Red Jacket* in sixty-three, sixty-seven and sixty-eight days respectively. And these were vessels twice the tonnage of the *Thermopylæ* !

What is the explanation? Simply this, obvious enough to sailormen, but not so easily grasped by landsmen agog for the marvellous.

These fabulous runs came into being from the custom of Yankee captains (legitimate enough in itself) of giving pleasure and encouragement to their passengers and enhancing the reputation of their ships, by stating that in the previous twenty-four hours the ship had traversed four hundred, or whatever it might be, miles.

It was not their business to explain to ignorant emigrants that miles of longitude were meant. And the omission of it has been responsible for some staggering yarns and impossible records among the credulous and romantic.

Running the easting down, below the 50th parallel of latitude—no infrequent course to be chosen in the days of Maury and Great Circle Sailing—a degree of longitude would not be more than about forty miles of actual distance. A ship, therefore, making, let us say, two hundred and eighty knots from noon to noon would cover seven degrees of longitude. As there are sixty miles of longitude to a degree, the vessel would have "covered" four hundred and twenty miles. In a word, nautical miles were confounded with miles of longitude to the infinite enhancement of the particular clipper's reputation.[1]

Consider, for a moment, what any other explanation would imply. There were quite a number of American flyers capable of doing round about four hundred and thirty miles in the twenty-four hours. Why did they all, and always, fail of making a passage commensurate with their speed? All other types of ships established records and made passages in accordance therewith. How comes it that the presumably fastest ships (by a long way) that ever floated, failed utterly and always to make a passage worthy of their speed? What can we think of the men who navigated them? Where is the Yankee energy and hard driving? If part of their passages were made at such a speed they must have dawdled shamefully for the rest of the time.

It would be all very interesting and exciting if, to a practical seaman, it were not rather absurd. The fact remains that the sailing-ships have yet to be built which could beat the pick of the later tea fleet for speed.

[1] Yet Captain Enright, as quoted by Mr. Basil Lubbock, specifically claims nautical miles and not miles of longitude. (Ed.)

rocks near Holyhead. Her crew took to the rigging and hung there for twenty-four hours, until the remnant of them were rescued by the Holyhead lifeboat.

That was the end of her sailing days; but as visitors to Falmouth may still see a tea-clipper with all her spars " a-taunt-o " in the shape of the *Cutty Sark*, so visitors to Anglesey may still see, defiant of wind and wave, the splendid iron frame of the *Norman Court*, half-buried and half-exposed, on the Welsh sands near Rhosneigr.

So the " tea-clipper " sleeps as the " tea-wagon " did before her, and as the great steamers will do after her, till the day comes when men desert the seas and travel among the clouds on the highways of the air.

> " Oh, the times was hard and the wages low,
>   Leave her, Johnny, leave her!
> You can pack your gear and go below,
>   It's time for us to leave her!

> " Oh, the grub has gone and the rats have too,
>   Leave her, Johnny, leave her!
> And it's time, my boys, that we went too,
>   It's time for us to leave her! "

INDEX